AN INTRODUCTION TO

PAINTING
STILL LIFE

AN INTRODUCTION TO

PAINTING
STILL LIFE

themes ● composition ● background ● light ● color

Peter Graham

BARNES & NOBLE BOOKS

NEW YORK

This edition distributed by Barnes & Noble Books

This edition published in 2004 by
CHARTWELL BOOKS
A Division of BOOK SALES, INC.
114 Northfield Avenue
Edison, New Jersey 08837
USA

This edition produced for sale in the U.S.A., its
territories, and dependencies only.

A QUINTET BOOK

Reprinted 2004

ISBN 0-7607-5845-x

This book was designed and produced by
Quintet Publishing Limited
6 Blundell Street
London N7 9BH

Creative Director: Terry Leavons
Designer: Wayne Blades
Project Editor: Sarah Buckley
Editor: Jenny Millington

Typeset in Great Britain by
Central Southern Typesetters, Eastbourne
Manufactured by Regent Publishing Services, Ltd.
Printed in Singapore by Star Standard Industries Pte Ltd.

CONTENTS

INTRODUCTION

For over 400 years, artists have explored the world of still life, and the results are astounding and varied. There has never been a better time to venture into still life: the contemporary artist can draw from a huge variety of rich traditions. Still life is experiencing a revival, with major exhibitions of the genre being held around the world.

A *historical perspective* The vibrant still life tradition in Spain, with its origins in the late 16th century, produced such painters as Velazquez (1599–1660) and Goya (1746–1828), who approached the still life in a truly independent way. Their influence has been far-reaching through history. It is evident in the works of artists spanning the centuries, through to Cézanne (1839–1906) and Picasso (1881–1973).

In the early 17th century, the reformed churches of northern Europe rejected the grandiose religious painting and decoration of the past. Artists had to find new ways of making a living. In Holland they turned to painting still life, and the great Dutch tradition was born. Here was an art that the Protestant Church could raise no objection to. The Dutch masters brought to still life their magnificently lavish ornamentation and wonderful draftsmanship. Today we marvel at the sheer mastery of technique of the Dutch

ABOVE Jan van Huysum, **"Still Life: a Vase of Flowers"** OIL. **Elaborate detail.**

ABOVE Velazquez, OIL. **"Peasants at Table" (detail) Early still life.**

painter Jan van Huysum (1682–1749), whose elaborate flower still lifes are best known for their "trompe l'oeil" effects, where an uncanny illusion of depth and realism is created: the triumph of the canvas over the eye.

In these still life paintings, artists were free to paint any objects they liked, and thus we see elaborate studies of Persian carpets, exotic fruits, and gleaming goblets. Painting that explored the sheer beauty of the visible world, and the objects in it was recognized as valid in its own right. Jan Vermeer (1632–75) was one of a number of artists to master this tradition. His seemingly effortless creation of texture, form and atmosphere paved the way for the great still life artists that followed.

The Dutch painter Vincent van Gogh (1853–90), born two centuries later, has captured the imagination of our generation. His violent yet harmonious compositions give the eye a new sensation. He lived in poverty, rejected by society and ridiculed for the crudity of his painterly technique. It was not until the later part of the 20th century that his work came to be recognized as totally innovative, and pivotal in establishing the direction that art would take from then on. He used the brush to convey his excitement for the paint: brushstrokes almost speak to the viewer of his torment and joy.

BELOW Vincent van Gogh, "Roses and Anemones" OIL. **Vivid color.**

The still lifes of the 19th-century French artists Matisse (1869–1954) and Cézanne are now acclaimed and revered. Cézanne, the father of Impressionism, employed a system of short, tightly grouped brushstrokes that is a technique employed today by many still life artists. His studio paintings were principally experimental efforts to achieve greater understanding of visual perception, to develop and construct a picture as a coherent totality of marks.

Henri Matisse's sensuous transformation into pigment of the simplest of compositions brings the surface of his canvasses to life, transcending anything before. As he said, "... Merely copying an object is not art. What counts is to express the emotion they call forth in you,

the feeling they awaken, the relations established between objects ...." The French Impressionist painter Edouard Manet (1832–83) transformed paint into flowers with his swift and lively brushstrokes: the paint became the flower. Van Gogh said of Manet's flower still lifes: "... as much a flower as anything could be, and yet painted in perfectly solid impasto."

The influence of the French Impressionists reached Britain and the Scottish Colorists, particularly F. C. Cadell (1883–1937) and S. J. Peploe (1871–1935). Alongside appreciation of color, they shared a bold and vigorous approach to brushwork. These painters produced magnificent still lifes. They took influences from the Impressionists, Cézanne, Matisse, Manet, and from Japanese art and design, and mixed it with the heritage of Scottish painters such as E. A. Hornell (1864–1933) and James Guthrie (1859–1930). Peploe's use of intense black to support objects and his masterly creation of planes of pure color, Cadell's composition, draftsmanship and color contrasts, bring to the viewer a new appreciation of the inner vision of the artist. Style rather than subject occupied these artists' minds: a shift away from the sentimentality and storytelling of earlier painters. The freshness and directness of the painterly approach of these Colorists has left a rich legacy for those who wish to follow.

ABOVE Paul Cezanne, "The Blue Vase" OIL. **The master of the still life.**

LEFT Edouard Manet, "Fleurs dans un Vase" OIL. **Expressive brushstrokes.**

The formal purity of the watercolor still lifes of the 19th-century Scottish painter and architect Charles Rennie Mackintosh (1868–1928) helped pave the way for the rich tradition of watercolor still lifes in Britain today. He did not follow the tradition, but preferred to be impressionistic, realistic, and scientific. Mackintosh loved pattern and symmetry, often painting backdrops echoing the shapes of his objects and flowers.

Picasso and Braque (1882–1963) brought a 20th-century method of representing perspective and depth. Picasso redefined volume while containing the integrity of the canvas. Tables tipped forward to reveal more of the objects, challenging the rules of perspective and taking still life further than any painter had dared.

ABOVE Peter Graham, "Art Deco Tulips" OIL.
In the tradition of the Scottish Colorists.

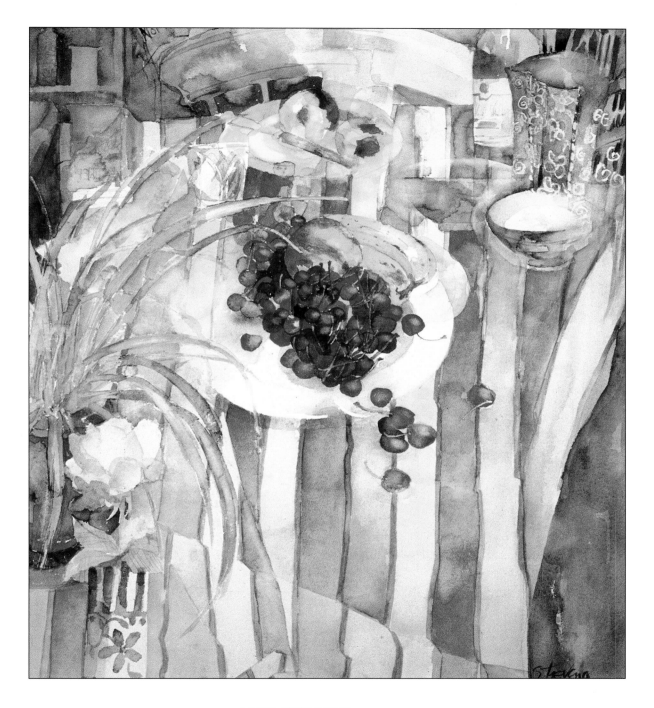

ABOVE Shirley Trevena,
"**Cherries on a White Plate**" WATERCOLOR.
Challenging the rules of perspective.

BECOMING A STILL LIFE ARTIST

Still life communicates to both artist and viewer. It can strongly convey emotions and feelings. It gives back to the viewer what the artist saw in the beginning. Consider that the first painting by Matisse was a still life, and feel your enthusiasm grow!

While working with still life, the artist has total control over everything in the painting. Still life is one of the most attractive of painting subjects: many artists enjoy the retreat to the studio, and work ferociously! This type of studio-bound work can, of course, be frustrating as well as addictive. Anything you choose to paint holds inherent problems—and still life has all of them. Without careful composition and attention

ABOVE Ronald Jesty, "An Ormer and other Seashells" WATERCOLOR. Inspiration from natural shapes and textures.

to drawing you can turn a potential masterpiece into a disappointment. Many artists approach still life by working monochromatically at first, and even working with collages of cut paper. This allows the artist to develop tonal values, composition, and then the use of color.

Draftsmanship is important, and developing this side of your work helps to free up the inspiration when it comes to the creative process. It is like playing the piano, where practice makes perfect! Studying composition is

also helpful. By constructing a still life perhaps with echoing shapes and related objects, you can lead the viewer's eye into and around the canvas from one focal point to the next. This book aims to clarify these issues, so as to enthuse, encourage, and satisfy your inner compulsion to paint! As with all reference books, you can pick and choose what parts you want to read. I can only scratch the surface of the subject here; I would like to show you a gallery of contemporary work that is leading us into the 21st century, and to encourage the painter to pick up those brushes and be inspired! The world is your oyster so why not paint them.

CHOOSING YOUR MEDIUM AND EQUIPMENT

F inding inventive ways of applying paint to paper, board, or canvas will turn a picture into a painting. Vigorously brushed textures, impressionist stippling, and rhythmic brushwork can bring your painting to life. Developing a fluent shorthand with painting and drawing takes time and experimenting with the various tools and media available is the best way to proceed. Buying painting and drawing media can be confusing when you are unsure about what will suit your purposes. It is easy to make expensive mistakes, so it is worth while to think carefully before buying.

WATERCOLOR

The great British tradition of watercolor has paved the way for the abundance of superior paints and pigments available throughout the world. This huge range of tints, tones, and hues gives the newcomer a bewildering array of choices. Artist's watercolor paint can yield superb results, even for the beginner, if handled properly. The subtlety of luminous washes and strong tinting qualities bring to the medium a vitality that lends itself to still life and flower work. Unfortunately the paint can be rather unforgiving, due to its transparency, but with practice the effects can be breathtaking.

The high-quality sets of watercolors you can buy often include colors that you personally may not use, so buy an empty paint box and make your own choice of colors. This will focus your mind on exactly what it is you are looking for (see pages 16–7).

GOUACHE

Gouache paints are opaque watercolor paints that come in tube form (see pages 16–7). They are opaque because of opaque extenders such as barium sulphate or chalk. The pigments are combined with gum and wetting agents to produce beautifully flowing colors.

Gouache, or "body color," can be used with watercolor to make excellent combinations of washes and opaque color, perfectly suited to flower still life work. This medium is also known as "designer's gouache," due to its ability to produce flat areas of matte color without brushmarks, which endears it to graphic designers. Gouache, as opposed to

ABOVE John Yardley, "May Blossoms" Still life in watercolors.

watercolor, is particularly suited to the student, because it is possible to rework and correct mistakes.

ACRYLIC

Acrylic paints (see pages 18–9) are water-based, non-yellowing permanent paints that dry to a waterproof finish. The acrylic medium is actually a plastic, made from petroleum products. The paints are user friendly, and there is a good choice of colors and hues.

BELOW A selection of drying oils and diluents for use in oil painting.

This flexible and fast-drying medium lends itself to layering techniques such as scumbling and transparent glazes. The fast-drying property also means that palettes and brushes must be carefully cleaned; if not, they can be easily ruined. There are superb mediums, such as gloss medium, matte medium, and gel medium, that can be used with the acrylic paint. Flow improvers, retarders, and impasto gels also give the artist a greater control over the nature and consistency of the paint. It is worth trying them all out.

OILS

The luminous quality of oil paint (see pages 20–1), and its ability to create glazes, thick impasto, and high contrasts, put it in a class of its own.

The huge range of colors and brands of oil paint available make the choice of a personal palette somewhat overwhelming. You may find that you prefer the consistency and handling of one brand, or certain colors of another, so leave your options open. Manufacturers usually give a choice of artist's or student's grades of paints, in both oil and watercolor. The "student"

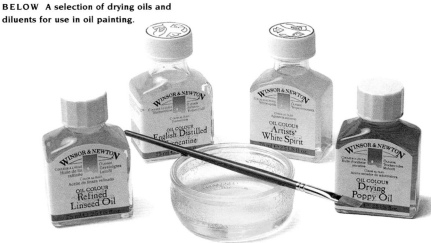

colors are slightly cheaper, but the pigments may be less concentrated or even substituted with alternatives, so that they do not achieve the brilliance of "artist" colors. That does not mean these paints are not worth using; in fact, they are excellent as a starter palette, when you are not sure of your commitment to the medium.

Refined linseed oil and *English distilled turpentine* (see opposite) are the only basic drying oil and diluent, respectively, that the artist in oils needs. A standard mixture of one-third linseed and two-thirds turps will serve the artist well. There are, however, many other mediums worth experimenting with. Synthetic mediums such as liquin will speed up drying time and will improve the flow of oil colors. It also increases translucency, making it suitable for glazes. Opal medium gives a matte appearance to colors and dries slowly. An impasto medium such as Oleopasto will give the brushstrokes more weight,

ABOVE Pastels are readily available in a whole spectrum of colors.

and the texture of the mark will be more exaggerated. This can also be used as an extender to make color go further. In this way it is possible to build up thick layers using minimal amounts of expensive paints. Artist's Retouching Varnish can be used to liven up dull, flat areas of a painting at the end of each day. You should experiment with the different types of oil and retouching varnish to find out if these mediums will benefit your own approach.

Drawing media

Producing a finished drawing of a still life, whether using dipper-pen and ink, colored pencil, oil, or soft pastel, or any of the great choice of media available, can be both informative and satisfying. Drawing can, of course, be used as a

preliminary step to painting (see Chapter 2), but it also represents a range of media that give excellent results in their own right.

The most commonly used drawing tools are pencil, conté, and charcoal. Charcoal is an expressive medium, allowing both fluid and accurate line and tone to be explored. It also dusts off fairly easily so that corrections can be made. Using a pencil to work out details and form is a very satisfactory method of working, as is conté crayon, which handles like a wax crayon, and makes the mark of compacted charcoal with none of the mess!

Soft pastel can be a perfect way into still life: you have the advantages of the glorious color without the need for all the paraphernalia that goes with painting. The soft painterly marks of these pastels, and the huge selection of colors that are available, make this a sensitive and responsive medium.

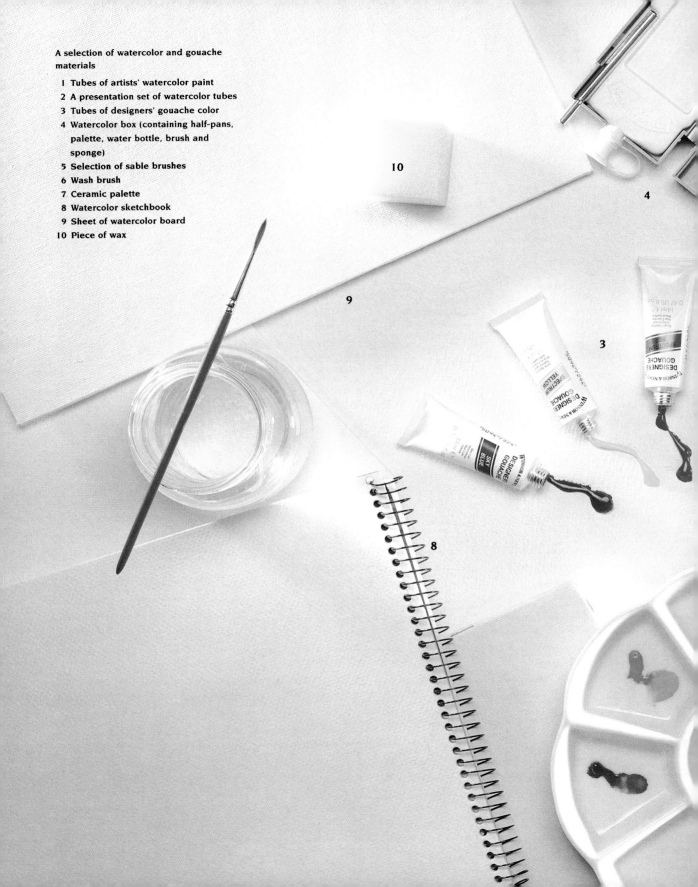

A selection of watercolor and gouache materials

1 Tubes of artists' watercolor paint
2 A presentation set of watercolor tubes
3 Tubes of designers' gouache color
4 Watercolor box (containing half-pans, palette, water bottle, brush and sponge)
5 Selection of sable brushes
6 Wash brush
7 Ceramic palette
8 Watercolor sketchbook
9 Sheet of watercolor board
10 Piece of wax

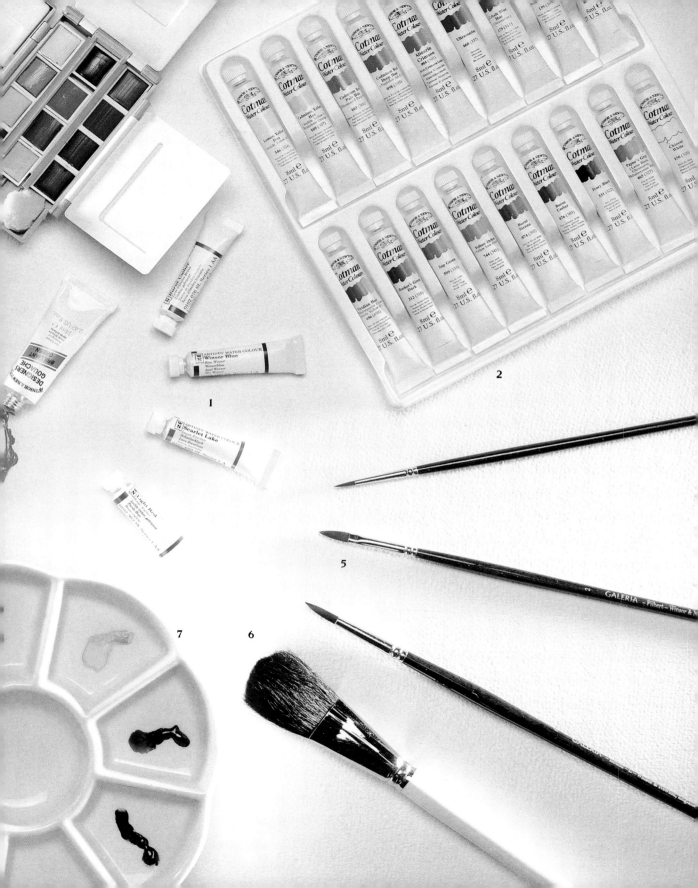

1

2

5

6

7

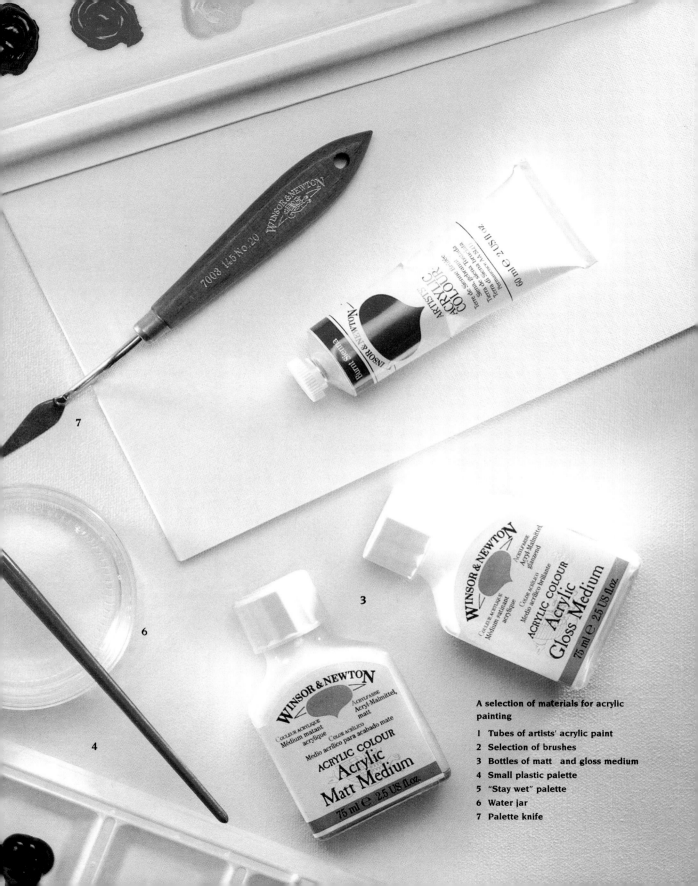

A selection of materials for acrylic painting

1 Tubes of artists' acrylic paint
2 Selection of brushes
3 Bottles of matt and gloss medium
4 Small plastic palette
5 "Stay wet" palette
6 Water jar
7 Palette knife

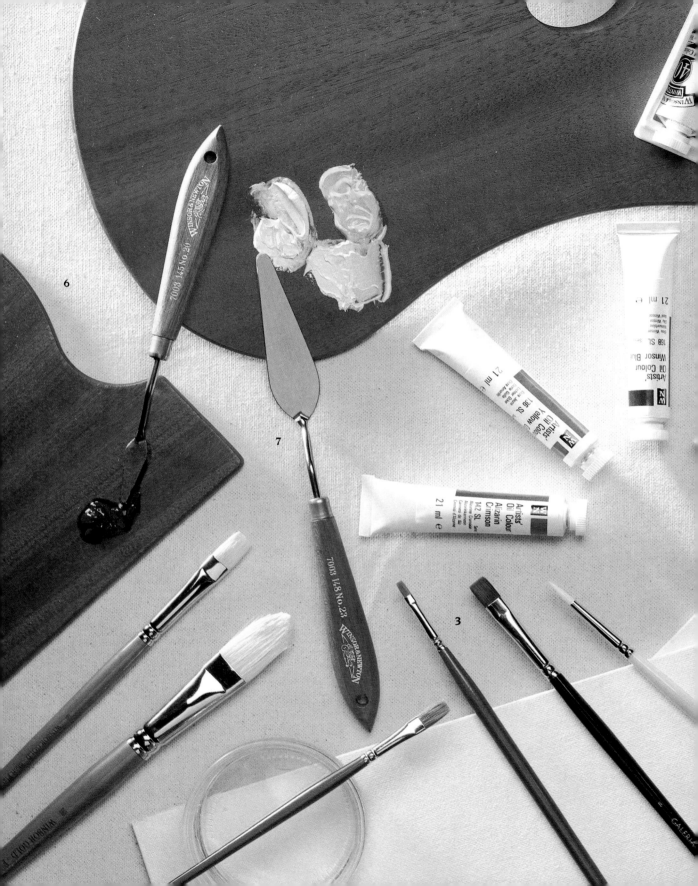

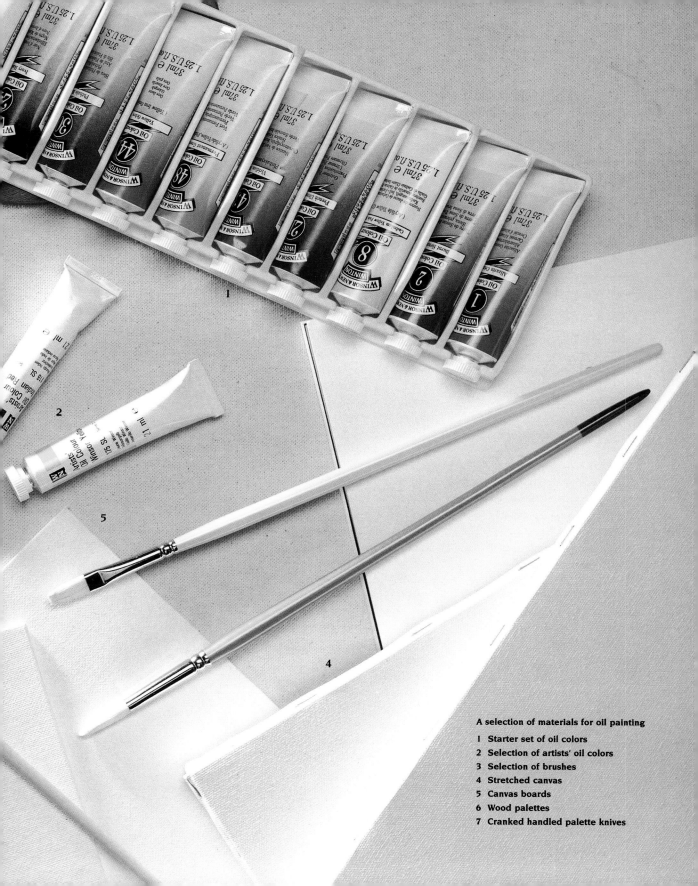

A selection of materials for oil painting

1 Starter set of oil colors
2 Selection of artists' oil colors
3 Selection of brushes
4 Stretched canvas
5 Canvas boards
6 Wood palettes
7 Cranked handled palette knives

Try out the many yellows and ochers, along with the more unusual green and blue tints, to experience the versatility of the medium. A pale rose or yellow instead of white, or burnt umbers or indigos instead of black, will help keep your work fresh as well as colorful.

Fixatives are important in order to protect the delicate surface of pastel. A simple hairspray does the job! Many pastel artists, however, prefer not to use fixative. Instead, they seal the drawing by mounting and glazing the work soon after completion.

EQUIPMENT

Palettes and accessories

Palettes The purpose of the palette is to display and mix the colors. The main palette for the studio-based artist can be a simple sheet of formica or heavy-duty glass, about two foot square, which sits on a table top next to the easel. Give yourself room to maneuver and get full use from your colors.

Disposable peel-off palettes are a fast and efficient way to mix lighter colors and try out experimental mixtures without taking up valuable space on the main palette. Washable plastic and enamel palettes, available in many shapes and sizes, are perfect for the studio-based watercolor or acrylic artist. It should be noted, however, that when using acrylic, it is very important to clean all the palettes meticulously before the paint starts to harden.

Dippers Dippers are the conveniently sized small metal containers for mediums such as the turps/linseed

mixture used by oil painters. I like to keep four of these going, with two for the light color brushes and two for the dark color brushes. This minimizes the chances of color contamination. I use a small jug of artist's white spirit, which is changed regularly, for brush cleaning.

Mahlsticks Painters use mahlsticks to keep the hand steady when working on awkward parts of the canvas or paper, and when executing precision or detail. The traditional mahlstick has one padded end, which gently rests on the painting surface, while the stick supports your arm.

Paper, board, and canvas

There is an abundant choice of excellent artist's papers for watercolor work, ranging from the "Ingres" tinted papers to Chinese handmade papers. Some top-quality papers are coated with a gelatin layer, which helps to prevent staining and increases the brilliance of washes. A good watercolor paper should not yellow over time and should be acid free. Paper thickness is measured in pounds or grams: the higher the number, the thicker the paper, and therefore the more durable (and the more expensive!). Artist's watercolor blocks, and the heavier weights of paper, do not necessarily require stretching.

A paper for watercolor (see page 23) must have a highly absorbent quality and be able to stand up to soaking, layering, and scraping techniques. The higher-quality papers are carefully treated in order to prevent them from rotting over a period of time, and to stop the watercolor soaking through the paper.

Traditionally the highest-quality papers are made from cotton fibers, which give the sheet strength and durability. The term "100% rag" is used to denote pure cotton fiber.

Papers come in three main categories. *Hot pressed* (HP) is smooth to the touch. *Cold pressed* (NOT) has a slight textural feel to it and is the ideal all-around paper to work on. *Rough* paper has a distinct tooth, which can produce magnificent results when used to full effect. A coat of size over stretched paper allows the artist to work with oils.

When it comes to choosing canvas or boards, the ready-made selection is very good. You can buy canvas primed and stretched, or you can buy canvas and stretchers separately. Textures from a strong coarse grain through to finely textured surfaces are available. To decide which kind of surface or canvas will suit you involves trial and error. A cotton duck canvas gives a good tooth for textured work, while still being capable of holding fine line and subtle washes of color. A fine linen canvas has a fine-grain surface suitable for high detail.

Brushes and other tools for applying paint

Brushes can create the mood of a painting, as shown by the swirling strokes of Vincent van Gogh or Edouard Munch (1863–1944), where raw emotions are expressed through vivid, energetic brushwork. Keep your brushwork free and lively, and you will see the benefits. Choosing the right brush for the right job means looking carefully at the selections in the art store. Know what kind of marks you want from your brush before trying some of them out.

You will need bristle brushes of various shapes and sizes, along with some sable brushes for precise detail and linework. Synthetic bristle-type brushes are also worth considering. They are hard-wearing and less expensive, and the range of shapes and sizes they come in gives the artist excellent choice and the chance to experiment. There are also less expensive alternatives to pure sable brushes, such as the synthetic mixtures that contain nylon or polyester. These brushes perform well and are especially suitable for beginners.

BELOW A selection of papers for watercolor painting.

The important thing to remember is to be confident with your brushwork, since this is the key to successful painting. A hesitant hand leads to caution and a reserved approach, which can stifle the creative process. Practice strokes with a dry brush to help the flow of thought to the hands, and allow rhythm and spontaneity to build up when handling the brush.

It is worth spending as much as you can afford on brushes, since these are the tools of the trade. The better the quality of the brush, the better it handles the paint!

Bristle brushes The hog-hair bristle brush itself is the ideal tool for mixing colors on your palette. The spring in the bristle is stiff enough for the paint to gradually work its way into the belly of the bristle. Always mix paint on the palette gradually, so that the bristles fill evenly with paint. There is nothing worse than an overloaded brush.

Filberts and *flats* are the most commonly used types of hog-hair bristle brush. Filberts are the all-around brush. The shape is flat with an oval head. A variety of textures, swirls, and tapered lines can be produced with filberts. This type of brush will deliver a good, even stroke of color, and is suitable for blocking in large areas of color in the early stages of a painting.

With their chisel heads, the "flat" brushes, with long or short bristles, make very distinctive diamond- or square-shaped marks, producing well-defined edges to your brushmark. The dappling effect produced with the flat was favored by the Impressionists. Their paintings clearly show deft brushstrokes flying across the canvas in an ordered chaos!

The *round* is ideal for outlines and for drawing out your composition. It is also good for stippling effects when held vertically. The larger rounds can also deliver wonderfully hefty brushstrokes, while still keeping a crisp edge, allowing a consistent flow of paint.

B*right* brushes are short, flat brushes, chisel-ended with a square head. They are useful for "scrubbing" paint into large areas of canvas, and they are durable enough to cope with vigorous, energetic handling.

The complete sets that have a "round," a "filbert," and a long and short "flat" selection are good to start with. A brush I use often for blending color is the *fan* brush. This comes in both bristle and soft hair.

Sable brushes Sables are soft hair brushes, especially suited to watercolors, although they are extremely useful to the oil painter as well. The finest quality sable, and the most expensive, is the Kolinsky sable, taken from the tail of the Siberian mink!

The sable tapers to a fine point, giving the artist precise control over the tip of the brush. It can be used for fine line as well as for precision painting and coloring. The responsiveness and color-carrying capacity of the sable are the main qualities that endear it to the artist. Watercolor is thin in consistency, so soft hair and sable brushes are the most suitable for it. Take care to avoid bending the hairs backward on these brushes, because this will shorten their life, and sables are not cheap! Good quality sables do not shed their hair easily, and if cared for, they will keep their shape (see Chapter 7).

Some manufacturers produce excellent ranges of sable brushes at reasonable prices, so shop around. In many ways, your choice of brush is personal to the way you paint, so experiment with less expensive brushes to find what type suits you. I use various sizes of Kolinsky sables and riggers (long, thin sables traditionally used for painting ships' rigging).

Mops and sponges There are many ways of applying paint. Especially useful for the watercolorist is an ox-ear-hair or squirrel-hair mop, used for flat washes, as is the goat mop. The natural sponge is also useful with water-based paints for creating special effects as well as moving the paint around.

Palette knives and painting knives Palette knives are useful for mixing large quantities of paint and so avoiding damage to brushes. The various palette and painting knives available give the painter another versatile range of tools. The palette knife can be used in both acrylic and oil painting for laying on paint like spreading butter, or for scraping off paint, creating textures as well as making corrections.

Artist's painting knives come in various shapes and sizes. The standard painting knife comes with a cranked wooden handle and a flexible steel trowel head. This shape is important as it allows the artist to work close to the surface of the canvas without leaning against it for support. The tip of the blade can be used to scrape back or draw into the paint. This sgraffito technique allows you to create different textures and also crosshatching, and this is described in detail in Chapter 8.

2

DRAWING, FORM, AND PERSPECTIVE

The development of powers of observation is vital in the search for self-expression through art. Looking toward the great Dutch tradition of meticulously careful drawing, and the Spanish mastery of observation, can yield great returns for the artist. Understanding the three-dimensional form is necessary before attempting to paint. Drawing out carefully, and looking at composition in terms of shapes and lines, takes some time to master, but pays off with results.

PRINCIPLES OF DRAWING

Cézanne was concerned all his life with the depiction of outline and how to draw a shape in a painterly manner. He would draw with pencil or brush, feeling for the outline of an object with numerous lines. He sought the underlying form of natural objects, as opposed to just their appearance. He called his works "constructions after nature." The French painter Pierre Bonnard (1867–1947) would grasp at a burned-out matchstick to capture a fleeting image or an effect of the light, and he would work on any scrap of paper he could lay his hands on. His creative impulse led him to feel drawing as pure sensation.

Observation

Drawing is basically a way of thinking about things. You may often see some new shape or tone in a glass vase the third time you draw it! Approaching drawing as a learning tool is a good start, producing a series of "studies" of compositions or objects. The whole process allows hand-eye coordination to develop, which then sharpens power of observation.

Many people are so concerned with correcting mistakes that the drawing board becomes a battlefield. Instead, learn from your mistakes. Erasing unsatisfactory drawing, only to repeat the mistake, will get you nowhere. It can be of great benefit to leave in the "mistakes" for your own reference in these studies.

It is important to recognize your own limitations and to try to think positively about your own particular vision of a subject. The discipline of observing and drawing regularly will lead to tangible improvement. Get into a routine and spend a couple of hours drawing each week.

Form

Before beginning a complicated painting of still life, it can be very worthwhile to make preparatory drawings of individual objects. You gain greater empathy with the objects, understanding ellipses, reflections, and form. When you go on to set up your composition, you will have absorbed the form and its idiosyncrasies. You thereby free up the inspiration to shine out.

**BELOW Oliver Soskice,
"Lime and Avocados"
Drawing capturing tone and line with charcoal.**

Keep your compositions restrained and simple at the early stages of the creative process. To start with simple understanding of shape and form leads the artist forward, channeling the flow of thought. Cézanne's theory of viewing still life as a sphere, cube, or cylinder encourages the mind's eye to see objects as real shapes: fruits as spheres, or vases as cylinders, and so on.

Tone

Tone describes the relative lightness or darkness of an area. Working monochromatically—with

ABOVE Nicholas Verrall, "Bottles against a Mirror"
A tonal approach allows the artist to emphasize the sculptural aspect of his subject.

only one color—allows you to observe and represent contrasts in a clear and precise manner. René Magritte (1898–1967) and Picasso both experimented with tonal still life. This has the effect of giving great weight to the objects. The sense of form is strong. Picasso visualized his objects and forms monochromatically. He felt color to be a separate process. His

approach was sculptural in a way. He would work in grays or blues, or tint his compositions like that of old photographs.

Relationships between objects

Within a still life, there are objects and then there are the spaces around them. These spaces can be seen as negative shapes. By observing negative shapes in the same way as the objects themselves, you will build up good spatial relationships between the objects, which is very important in the composing of still life.

The illusion of spatial depth is heightened by objects overlapping each other and projecting in front of or behind the frame. In a painting that has objects in a row, the viewer sees very little depth. This effect can be an advantage, creating a calm horizontal pattern. If the objects overlap, however, we can have a much better idea of spatial relationships between them.

In life, most objects that we see are partly obscured by others, and in our mind's eye we make up the rest of the shapes ourselves. In still life painting this type of "seeing" is one of the keys to making an exciting composition and creating depth within the confines of the canvas. When you use the simple devices of size, position, and overlap in drawing the composition, you provide the viewer with all the clues necessary to understand the image. In the mind's eye, highly complex spatial relationships can be recreated.

Perspective

Perspective is a method by which an artist commits to two dimensions the illusion of three. Traditionally, perspective is associated with landscape painting, but it is also very important to the still life artist, even when drawing the shape of an individual object. Perspective helps to insure that objects in the composition are recognizable to the viewer.

With linear perspective, the further away an object lies, the smaller it will appear in the composition. This can be shown using parallel lines that eventually recede towards vanishing points. The rules of perspective place the viewer in one position, so when building up a composition it is

PERSPECTIVE ILLUSTRATED BY RICHARD SELL

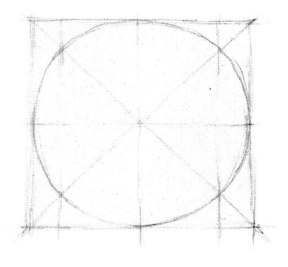

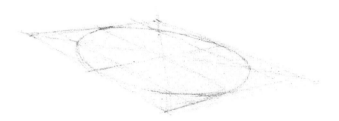

TOP Circles and ellipses come up constantly in still life objects. Drawing a square and then a circle within helps the artist to draw a circle accurately by approaching it in quarter sections.

RIGHT In this composition one can clearly see how Richard Sell has handled the complicated set of ellipses to give a real sense of volume to the glasses. Note the perspective, which places one apple and one glass higher in the frame, creating the illusion of depth. The device of overlap also creates depth, as clearly shown by the apple in the foreground partly obscuring the bottom of the glass.

LEFT Here the ellipses of a teakettle are achieved by drawing a cube, with parallel horizontal lines meeting at their vanishing points on the horizon. Note that the center of the teakettle has an imaginary vertical line drawn up from the center of the base circle.

essential that you observe the subject from a precise spot, so as to preserve the same vanishing points. Remember that parallel horizontal lines have their vanishing points on your eye level, the same as the horizon.

Manipulating perspective and using it where appropriate is generally accepted in the genre. Being creative with perspective has excellent advantages in describing to the viewer unique relationships between objects, and in shifting focus from one point to the next.

UNDERDRAWING IN PREPARATION FOR PAINTING

To produce an underdrawing (see left) is simply to sketch out the composition and suggest tonal differences. This can be carried out using either pencil, conté, or even charcoal, for example.

Artists can often go overboard with detail when producing an underdrawing of the composition. When the painting commences, all that hard drawing work is painted over and lost. It is best to keep the underdrawing to a minimum. Some artists like to prepare a small-scale drawing of a composition and then carefully scale it up to their canvas.

You may prefer to use a brush for the underdrawing. The flowing, confident lines of a brush can sit quite comfortably under washes of paint, and may even show in places in the finished painting. This does not mean that careful observation and the understanding of perspective should be ignored.

The golden rule is patience. The more accurately you observe the relationships between objects at this early stage, the easier it becomes to go on and take the painting to a successful conclusion.

DAFFODILS

Underdrawing for a painting in oils

J E R E M Y   G A L T O N

Working from an underdrawing allows you to paint with more confidence, and reduces the risk of having to make corrections. This underdrawing by Jeremy Galton shows how the composition is transferred from real life on to a two-dimensional surface.

PALETTE

French ultramarine: Winsor blue: sap green: raw sienna: raw umber: burnt umber: cadmium yellow: lemon yellow: Winsor violet: titanium white.

1 These beautiful spring daffodils were the inspiration for this still life in oils.

2 Using a pencil on a ground washed with raw sienna, the artist starts the underdrawing in the center of the picture with the glass vase and flower heads.

3 Jeremy uses a ruler to work out the precise measurement of each object as seen from his chosen viewpoint, and then transfers the measurement to the two-dimensional board.

4 The underdrawing becomes the foundation for the painting to follow. Accuracy at this stage is desirable, although it is important not to overwork the drawing.

5 Jeremy Galton uses his method of color matching, painting a scale of color on a palette knife and selecting the particular hue that is required. Here, the artist is able to judge subtle differences within each petal.

6 The artist's working method here is to paint each component part of the composition, following the underdrawing closely. The flower petals are painted precisely, using a small sable brush.

7 A combination of detailed underdrawing and carefully matched colors brings to life this simple composition of garden apples and daffodils.

3

SELECTING
A SUBJECT

Be prepared to spend some time deliberating and contemplating your choice of subject and source of inspiration. You may be inspired by Moorish architecture, eastern European folk art, surface texture and pattern, intertwined with classical shapes, pitchers, and bowls. Evoke the seasons: spring and its apple blossom, fall and its warm colors or harvest and fruitfulness, winter and its black silhouettes.

INSPIRATION

Still life inspiration can come from any source. The common language of the genre starts with the depiction of familiar objects. Plain is beautiful: fruit and flowers, bowls and pitchers, sitting against a patterned background, an interior, or window. You only have to look at the enormous interest in the still life paintings of the past to realize that it is more than simple arrangements of objects we are dealing with here. Pictures can capture deep-running emotions or the spirit of a time, while communicating with the viewer on the freshest, simplest level.

The early still lifes had set rules: a table of objects, with an obscured, normally dark backdrop, very little depth of field, and lots of clear defined textures. The composition would lead the eye in an upward direction, diagonally across the surface of the canvas.

**LEFT Shirley Trevena,
"Blue China" WATERCOLOR.
Inspired by color and classical forms.**

**ABOVE Nicholas Verrall,
"The Dresser, Morning Light" OIL.
Evoking summer sun.**

**RIGHT James McDonald,
"1971, Herald" OIL.
An unusual choice of subject.**

LEFT Jenny Wheatley,
"Tropical Interior"
Curling brushstrokes link all the
component parts of the picture.

RIGHT Peter Graham,
"Afternoon Tea" OIL.
A visual theme of swirling shapes running
through the composition.

BELOW Arthur Easton, "Still Life
with Kettle and Ball of String"
A curious balance is attained in this
unusual composition.

These safe and predictable geometric rules of composition sometimes stifle inspiration. Rules are made to be broken, and when searching for individual response to your subject, breaking rules may be the only way forward. These days anything goes: some extraordinary subjects are painted, and inspiration is vital to the creative process. If old pots and pans or the most exotic fruit inspire you to put brush to canvas, then go with the flow.

Look hard at the objects to allow the brain to decipher their color. In this way, what appears to be a muddy brown could become a red tone, a dark shadow a purple. The warm and cool qualities of light and shade are one of the keys to recognizing underlying color. The optical effect of certain colors bring dynamism to a composition that otherwise may be a mundane selection of objects. Still lifes can be soaked in color, with dancing light creating pattern, depth, and form.

Consider the symbolic approach to flowers used by Renoir (1851–1919), where the rose was a symbol of feminine beauty, or the Dutch symbolic inclusion of history books, or a glass on its side to remind us of the fleeting nature of things. Still life can include symbols of vanity, the musical instrument; butterflies, expressing the free spirit; a lemon, beautiful to look at, bitter to taste, symbolising a deceptive appearance; red, with its theatrical connotations. Picasso used symbolism constantly in his still life work: a bowl of peaches representing his mistress, and guitars as symbols of the male.

STILL LIFE WITH ORANGES

Painting in oils

ARTHUR EASTON

This unusual still life composition is handled using muted tones and crisp detail, drawing very much from the Dutch tradition.

PALETTE

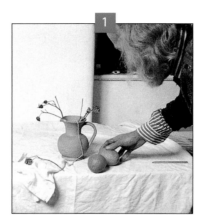

1 Dried flowers, a plain jug, white drapes and oranges might seem an unusual choice for a still life, but Arthur Easton takes advantage of the subtlety of contrast to breathe life into this scene.

Alizarin crimson: burnt sienna: cadmium red: yellow ocher: chrome yellow: titanium white: French ultramarine: viridian: sap green.

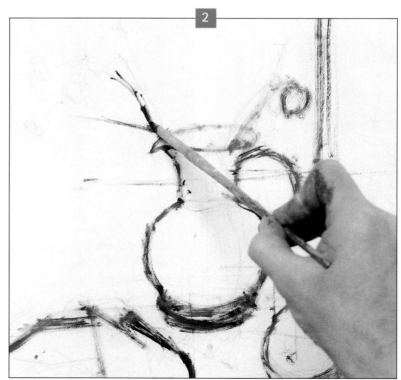

2 Arthur uses a small filbert bristle brush to draw out his composition. A mixture of burnt sienna and ultramarine combine to produce a clear, distinct outline.

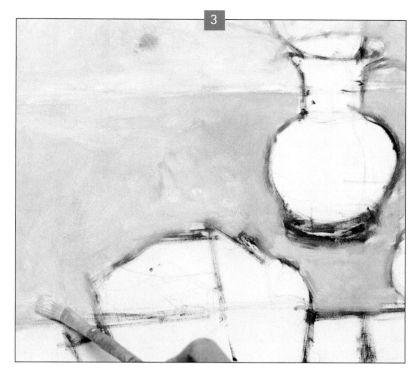

3 Using a large filbert, the background tones are laid down. The color is a mixture of titanium white, ultramarine blue, and burnt sienna.

4 The jug is the dominant object in the group, and is being built up first in order to anchor the composition.

5 Great care is taken to keep all the contrasts in harmony, since this is a key compositional element to this painting.

6 A "rigger" sable brush is used to pick out the spindly stems.

7 At this stage, the general form of the composition is complete. The artist can now think about contrasting the solid objects with the fine detail of the dried roses and drapery folds.

8 The highlight on the white drape in the foreground is painted with a filbert brush.

9 Smaller details like the glint on the neck of the jug are now added.

10 The orange peel is carefully picked out, using a small sable. The textural detail of all the objects plays an important role in keeping the painting lively.

11 The artist now adds final touches to the stark backdrop, taking care not to disturb the subtle balance of contrasts and focal points.

12 In the finished painting you can see the gentle folds and soft shadows of this simple grouping of objects transformed into an exquisitely delicate composition.

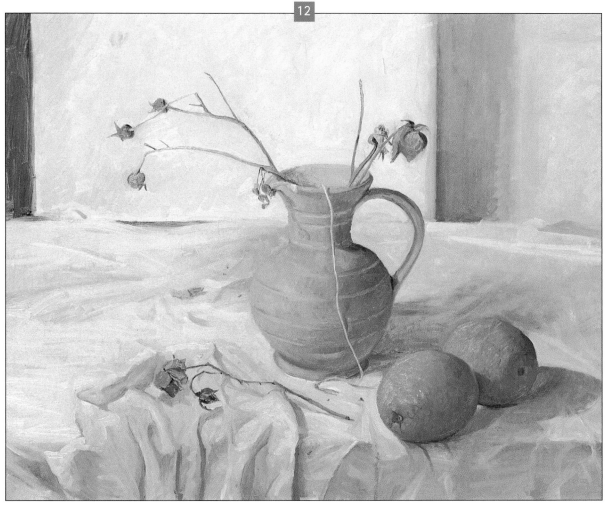

ABOVE Peter Graham,
"Mixed Fruits" OIL.
**A natural chaos of fruits being painted
where they fall.**

CHOICE OF OBJECTS AND THEMES

Still lifes have to start somewhere: a favorite vase, an intricately patterned carpet, a favorite color. Use these initial ideas and build on them. You can gradually develop your still life step by step.

I prefer a "natural chaos" theory, paying particular attention to the compatibility of color. This means placing objects and drapes in various positions and using a viewfinder, which is a small window mount cut in the same shape as your canvas, to make decisions about the composition and the color balance.

I can sometimes spend a day or two moving objects around. I even find myself going out to the local antique stores and markets to look for that certain something: a cup, a coffeepot, a scarf, that will lift and inspire the composition. This means that my studio is now full of unusual bits and pieces. Keep your

eyes open at friends' houses too—
they just might lend you their
favorite vase!

ABOVE James McDonald,
"Lawn mower, Millhall Farm"
Individual response using
gouache.

Flowers

Nature is a great source of ideas for
color and shape. For flower
arrangements, the simple selection
of country flowers is often the
answer to a composition. A simple
random element will lift the

painting out of the ordinary. Look
at the way flowers sit in nature.
Take notes of the color contrasts in
summer and fall, and combine
these with the wonderful natural
colors available in fabric to
transform your ideas into an
exciting composition. The sheer
precision of color in anemones, or
the exquisite blue of a cornflower.
can lead the artist into wonderful
contrasting juxtapositions of color
while keeping a naturally balanced
palette.

Think of all the other elements
that the flowers will be sitting
beside, and the backdrop of color.
The mood of a painting is set with
the flowers. Roses are excellent
subjects to paint, but they tend to
change shape and wilt fairly rapidly,
so you must observe carefully and
work quickly.

I like painting chrysanthemums: they are irregularly shaped flowers with a bright head of linear petals. The appearance of the flower lasts, and they tend to stay in one place in the vase! Similarly, daisies have a good strong color and shape to paint, and I find them a very flexible flower to use, since they last a long time and they present wonderful possibilities for precise brushwork.

Mixtures of flowers can pull together colors in different parts of the painting. A yellow daisy will pick up a tone from a yellow drape, a pattern of petals will reflect a design on a bowl.

Flowers presented in glass vases or unusual pitchers, and combined with fruit, make a favorite subject. They are not, however, the easiest of subjects to paint. Overworking

ABOVE Philip Sutton, "Natasha's Flowers" OIL. Color and natural shapes.

the paint in order to describe a flower's delicate structure is a common problem. Simplify what you are looking at, and capture the essence of a flower as opposed to making a copy. It is worth while, however, to study the flowers you

are going to paint, for example to discover how many flower heads there are to each stem. An understanding of a particular flower's shape and texture will leave you more informed when it comes to putting brush to canvas. Achieving good results in painting flowers takes hard work and perseverance, bearing in mind that no two flowers are alike. However, a few disappointments along the way are a small price to pay in learning to paint these rewarding subjects.

LEFT John Yardley, "Sunlit Blooms" Chrysanthemums back lit.

ABOVE Peter Graham, "Japanese Print with Flowers" OIL.
Still life with an Oriental theme.

VISUAL THEMES

A combination of objects can be chosen for their shape or appearance. For example you could choose an "art deco" theme, with angular arrangement of drapery and period ceramics, or an oriental theme with Japanese areas of pure color. Or have a circular theme: plates, apples, oranges, patterns on drapes or bowls. Fruit is a perfect subject to paint, as the textures, reflections and shapes have a natural beauty about them, and the rhythm of curves can balance in ways that other subjects cannot.

To relate objects by adopting a distinctive manner of brushstrokes, as in Cézanne's work, is a good way of linking and unifying composition.

RIGHT Jenny Wheatley, "Ironstone" Pattern running through the composition.

Peter Graham, "Deco Still Life" OIL. An Art Deco theme.

The simplicity and directness of this approach can bring power and presence even to the most mundane of objects, white drapery, pots, or glasses.

The eye should be directed from one object to another, and relationships need to be established. Devices such as overlapping shadow, or objects sitting in front of others, strengthen the unity of the whole surface.

Bear in mind the technique employed by Charles Rennie Mackintosh of designing and painting his own backdrops, or the Cubist method of artificially tipping objects forward so that you see the ellipse of a cup or plate.

ABOVE Peter Graham, "Vase of Anemones" OIL. Emphasizing natural shapes and textures.

BELOW David Napp,
"Summer Harvest"
The "Found" still life.
A sunlit table captured
with pastel.

ABOVE Ronald Jesty, "Pear on a Plate" A single pear painted in watercolor.

Single object

The painting of a single object set on a table has been favored by many artists. Such painters as William Nicholson (1872–1949) loved the gleam of a gold cup or the polished surface of a stoneware jar. Achieving a sophisticated simplicity within still life is a difficult task, so do not assume that this is an easy option!

Narrative themes

A narrative theme can be introduced into the still life. This can involve painting personal possessions or objects that evoke special memories. Van Gogh's paintings of his own boots is an example. This personal approach to subject can be a very fulfilling theme to follow through.

Found still lifes

A kitchen corner or garden shed may hold wonderful color and composition, and can lead to the most exciting still lifes. These chance compositions are known as "found still lifes." It may be that the breakfast table or dresser top hold possibilities for painting. Keep your artistic hat on all the time to recognize the found still life when it presents itself!

4

COMPOSITION

Composition is probably the most important element for successful still life painting. Still life arranging is like composing an imagined landscape. A combination of restraint and enthusiasm is needed. Objects are related through association, and this relationship forms the basis for the harmony within the picture. Still life painting involves themes and connections between objects, colors, and textures. Compositional tools can pull together the picture area. Where composition fails, confusion takes over.

ABOVE Philip Sutton,
"The Painting Flowers of Heather Sutton"
Still life composition in oil.

VISUALIZING THE COMPOSITION

"The whole arrangement of my picture is expressive. The place occupied by objects, the empty spaces around them, the proportions, everything plays a part. Composition is the art of arranging in a decorative manner the various elements at the painter's disposal for the expression of his feelings"—Henri Matisse. In order to build vocabularies of images, many artists will keep piles of drawings and sketchbooks in their studios. Keeping notes and sketches is very important for the nurturing of thoughts. One of the most interesting parts of creating a piece of work is the way you follow through an idea that develops in your head. I may find that a pattern in a cloth, or an interesting

ABOVE Peter Graham,
"Still Life, Pink Roses" OIL.
A delicate balance.

RIGHT Thumb-nail sketches are useful
for expanding ideas.

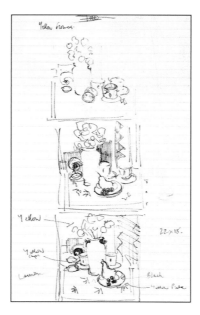

color contrast in nature, can set off ideas. Then I sit with a sketch-pad and try to work through my thoughts with lots of little sketch notes (below left).

You may find it difficult to visualize how the setup will look once it is on your canvas. To imagine the three-dimensional setup on a two-dimensional plane, a "viewfinder" comes in handy. This allows you to visualize the composition on the canvas and set your parameters.

Some artists prefer to block in all the component parts of a composition, and complete the final work on the background after all other objects have been painted: others work with the whole composition at the same time.

Central verticals, similarity of shapes and sizes, high contrasts, and strong diagonals like the edge of a table or drape can lead the eye to where you want it to go. Some of the French Impressionist painters, for example Pierre Bonnard, introduced vertical and horizontal stripes in the form of checked tablecloths or window frames in order to strengthen their compositions. Crowded groupings of objects and flowers against a dark background can lead to an excellent composition.

There are painters who create their own compositions directly on the canvas, referring to individual objects as and when they want to. Picasso and Braque would do this while composing their Cubist still life tables.

The objects in a still life are usually represented within a shallow picture space. Rules of perspective still apply, but they are not as obviously apparent as in the other types of picture. Using a

dynamic perspective creates scale: for example, taking the artificial viewpoint of an ant would make objects appear huge, and the vanishing points of the converging lines of perspective might only be slightly further into the picture plane than the objects themselves.

Successful paintings have a visual balance. This can be achieved by careful use of shapes, color, perspective, lines, and textures. The use of a strong vertical in the painting acts as an anchor for the composition, giving stability, weight, and structure. Also, the "art of leaving out" becomes an essential ingredient in selecting, designing, and composing your painting.

ABOVE Ronald Jesty, **"Time for Reflection"** WATERCOLOR. **An unusual view point.**

BOUQUET WITH FRUIT

Oil on board

P E T E R   G R A H A M

This still life in oils brings life to the whole surface of the canvas. Highly patterned drapes, contrasting fruits, and china give an ideal opportunity to create a dazzling combination of style, color, and content.

PALETTE

Lemon yellow hue: Winsor lemon: cadmium yellow: aureolin: Naples yellow: Mars yellow: raw sienna: terra rosa: raw umber: alizarin crimson: cadmium red: cadmium scarlet: permanent rose: cobalt violet: French ultramarine: indigo: cadmium green: Winsor green: Prussian green: titanium white

1 This arrangement of objects has been carefully placed to bring out pattern, leading the eye gently around the colors, shapes, and forms. Yellow shades in the flowers are reflected in the drapes, cups, and lemon, and this is complemented by green shades running through the apples, limes, and foliage.

2 Large flats and filberts are used to lay down areas of thinned oil paint. Lemon yellow hue and Mars yellow form the basis for the predominantly warm background.

3 The general colors are blocked in, and key lines and compositional details have been added; for example, the vase and the edges of the cups. This is treated in a very loose manner, which helps give the painting life and vigor right from the start.

4 The darker tones are applied, building up the color gently. Here the green foliage is being painted with swift chisel marks from a flat bristle brush.

5 The negative shapes between flowers are painted, keeping a crisp edge for the petals of the flowers. Prussian green, umber, and sienna are used to increase the depth of contrast.

6 The bouquet is outlined using thick, bold brush marks, and the patterned drape in the foreground has been painted with distinct brushwork over the color washes of previous stages. The composition is taking shape.

7 The use of a painting knife to draw the edge of the vase is a way of emphasizing its shape.

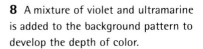

8 A mixture of violet and ultramarine is added to the background pattern to develop the depth of color.

9 The composition is virtually complete. All that remains is the attention to detail.

10 A large, round (no. 10) sable is used to pick out the black handles and decoration on the cups. A clean, swift stroke leaves a good line of color.

11 The gloss on the grapes is achieved, again using a sable, with mixtures of indigo, violet, and titanium white. The outline of the grapes is "drawn" carefully with a painting knife.

12 The resulting painting uses color and pattern to lead the viewer in and around the whole surface.

BUILDING THE COMPOSITION

Lighting

Natural light The ideal light for the studio is a diffuse north light. This casts no well defined shadows, and the tones remain constant throughout the day. Light falling on an object creates color. If you work in a naturally bright studio, as seen in art schools with their walls of windows, you will have the best opportunity of making informed decisions about color.

Alternatively you may be inspired by the effects of sunlight and may be prepared to work fast! It can be exhilarating to try and capture the dappling effect of sunlight on a table. The interplay of shadow can lead the eye and counterbalance the objects themselves.

Working in the house or garden with "found still lifes" can be challenging, due to the fleeting nature of sunlight. The dramatic effects of the sun and strong shadow are excellent ways of unifying color and form. Short sessions of "alla prima" painting, laying wet paint on wet paint, are one way of achieving a sunlit painting. Returning at the same time each day and working in sunlight requires discipline. Be careful not to alter the lighting and composition inadvertently as the light changes. A typical error would be the inconsistency of the shadow-angle cast by objects.

A vase of flowers on a windowsill, lit from the window behind, can create wonderful contrasts and natural compositions. Exaggerated shadow and silhouetted shapes from backlit subjects can enhance the composition, and the subtle interplay of grays and whites can produce satisfying results.

ABOVE Nicholas Verrall, "Still Life with Decoy Ducks"
The fleeting nature of sunlight captured in oils.

SUMMER HAZE
Pastel drawing

D E R E K   D A N I E L L S

Derek Daniells captures a sunlit patio, using soft pastels on tinted Ingres paper.
Sunshine delicately reflecting off the flowers and terracotta pots brings to this
"found still life" a wonderful sense of light, shade, and depth.

PALETTE

Cadmium orange: Lemon
yellow: Hooker's green
medium: Hooker's green light:
raw sienna: yellow ocher:
indigo: purple: lemon yellow
medium: terra verte: pansy
violet: Naples yellow: blue
green: cobalt light: cobalt
medium: crimson lake:
reddish purple: silver white.

1 Having carefully mapped out the whole composition, just suggesting the color, the artist starts to lightly sketch in the negative shapes and the main plant pots.

2 The pastel drawing is now taking shape, and all the groundwork and positioning decisions have been made.

3 In order to create depth and tone, Derek is applying the pastel in small dashes, capturing tiny amounts of color in the tooth of the paper.

4 The layering ability of pastel allows colors to be placed one on top of another, as demonstrated here, to create the dappled effect of shadow on the background foliage.

5 The color is carefully judged to keep the delicate contrasts in harmony.

6 The whole picture is gradually building up, strengthening in intensity, at a steady pace.

7 A stippling effect for the sunlit path allows the base color of the tinted paper to reflect through the lemon yellow and silver white veil of color.

8 The soft transitions of color that can be attained with pastel are brought to full effect in the completed work.

Artificial light There are times when it is unavoidable to work under artificial light. Also many artists prefer to work at night. You should realize, however, that ordinary artificial light causes a yellow cast, which will affect your colors. Using "daylight" neon or tungsten bulbs gets around that problem.

The best way to light a subject is with a strong, indirect light source. Reflecting light off ceilings or walls is a good way of dispersing it to give a good illumination to the subject. You also need to light your canvas separately, so that you can see clearly what you are doing. An adjustable lamp on the painting table is a good idea.

Experimenting with different forms of lighting can lead to a fuller understanding of composition. Always bear in mind that dramatic lights and darks can bring out the still life to full effect.

ABOVE John Yardley, "**Peony Tulips and Silver Teapot**" OIL. **Shadows and silhouetted shapes.**

BELOW Jeremy Galton, "**Still Life**" OIL. **A diffuse north light gives an even tone.**

Background

The artist has to think carefully about background: this will probably take up most of the canvas area. The aim is to achieve harmony and balance between the different elements within the picture frame. Draped fabric is a traditional method of bringing color and contrast to a background. Look for drapes that you like and that form themes or links with your objects, through either color or shape. A repeated pattern that echoes a shape within a flower or object can successfully create a bond between the subject and the background. You could even design and make your own backdrop.

Take care not to undermine the main focal point by creating too strong a contrast elsewhere in the composition. For example, the power of a red drape or dark shadow will affect the focus and composition of the painting.

A table set against a dark, plain backdrop, with the back edge of the table obscured from the viewer, is a traditional approach. This backdrop of darkness has the advantage of making an accurate measurement of depth nearly impossible. The viewer is given an ambiguous impression, which adds a magical quality to a painting.

Plain drapes can be the perfect foil for a complicated subject, but the treatment of these areas can let a painting down unless you are careful. Techniques such as scumbling or the use of broken color can keep large areas of plain colored drapes alive. Background areas are dominant with still life, so exaggerating textural and tonal contrasts will help the overall compositional structure.

ABOVE Peter Graham, **"Breakfast Still Life"** OIL. Still life with a dark blue drape backdrop.

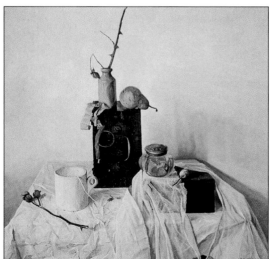

RIGHT Arthur Easton, **"Stone Jar, Cup and Withered Rose"** OIL. A plain background can be very effective.

Matisse was able to capture intense but very simple color harmonies on a vast scale. He tended to use his own studio for his large still life backgrounds. This gave his work a greater depth, and kept the visual excitement by using large areas of color to describe walls or canvasses in the studio. He was also creating pattern on a grand scale. He was the master of placing objects within a huge picture plane, purely to stimulate the harmony of the composition and to balance his own extraordinary color contrasts.

ABOVE Peter Graham,
"The Cherry Pot" OIL.
Dark objects next to light to create depth and contrast.

Focal point

Focal points within the composition hold the structure together. Try using the "rule of thirds" when placing your objects within the composition. Divide the canvas into thirds, both horizontally and vertically. Balanced focal points exist where the gridlines cross. These spots are good places to locate the centers of interest, whether they are a vase,

flowers, an unusual pattern, or exotic fruit. Keep an open mind, though: some obscure compositions can be surprisingly successful.

Counterchange

This is an excellent technique for leading the viewer to the focal points. It involves placing dark objects next to light objects and vice versa, creating dynamic contrasts, each leading in turn to the next. Keep the most exciting contrasts for the very center of attention.

ABOVE Jeremy Galton, "The Copper Pot" OIL.
Still life composition that uses the rule of thirds.

SHAPE AND SIZE OF THE CANVAS

The shape of support you work on will determine the type of composition you will end up with, so give some thought to this area. "Portrait" shaped canvasses can lead the eye upward through the composition, while a "landscape" format can emphasize the horizontal aspect of your subject.

The choice of shape and size is limitless, and experimenting within this area gives a new freedom to the painter. The square has wonderful visual powers of containing the eye, and can reveal new and exciting compositional qualities. Many galleries now hold exhibitions specifically for small still lifes,

ABOVE Anthony Green, "The Still Life Painter" OIL. A shaped canvas giving a unique perspective.

ABOVE Peter Graham, "Flowers and Grapes" OIL. Square shaped composition.

and this has become a category of work accepted in its own right. Working small has many advantages; there is less area to cover, and therefore fewer compositional difficulties. Working on a large scale is both daunting and exhilarating. A large blank canvas gives an enormous freedom to the artist, but dealing with vast areas of tone and texture can take many hours of balancing and reshaping before a strong composition reveals itself. When the composition is balanced, the impact is monumental. Large works take on a life of their own, dominating the environment in which they hang.

TOP Jenny Wheatley,
"Gold Filigree" WATERCOLOR AND GOLD.
Lattice gold work unifies the composition.

ABOVE Sandy Murphy, "Orchid and
Orange Frieze" INK AND ACRYLIC.
A band of orange binds the composition
together.

Decorative devices

Bands of color, or complete frames
within frames, painted as part of a
composition, are excellent for
balancing the picture as a whole.
This technique, used extensively by
Matisse, is a simple decorative

device that can add color, pattern,
and structure to a painting. Also, to
"frame" a subject with flowers or
drapery around the edge of the
work contains the eye, and
naturally draws the focus into the
body of the piece.

**ABOVE Philip Sutton, "Flowers from Battersea"
A bright still life in oils.**

**TOP RIGHT Peter Graham,
"Table of Magical Fruits" OIL.
Decorative devices contain the eye.**

When tight controls on the picture are abandoned, this does not necessarily lead to disaster. Drawing on the theories of Cézanne, the artist may freely allow color to suggest form and light. To convey a sense of unity and build relationships within the canvas through fluid brushwork, flickering color, or a limited palette provides unique structures and parameters in which to express emotion and feelings in your paintings.

Managing to create the feeling of light and air in your painting, through the use of strong compositional elements, can be extremely rewarding so it is well worth spending some time trying out different and new ideas. To experiment is a necessary part of painting, and the success or failure of an individual painting should not be the main concern.

FINALIZING THE COMPOSITION

There comes a point with all pictures when a balance is struck between all the constituent parts. Every object and form has found its definitive relationship. When a painting appears to light up from within, the composition comes to life. This state is created by internal contrasts and subtle color balances. This delicately orchestrated world of paint allows the tiniest mark to open up whole new relationships within a painting. From this point on, to alter even the smallest part can dramatically change the balance of the work.

5

COLOR, LIGHT, AND SHADE

A richness of colors delight the spirit. To be able to translate our personal vision onto paper and canvas is why we paint. To use the language of paint, through to the different techniques at our disposal, is part of the whole process. The wider your range of technical ability, the easier it becomes to express yourself through color and paint.

Cézanne's theory was that the more the colors sit in harmony, the more the outline stands out, so when color is at its peak, form reveals itself to us. Color can also be harnessed to evoke periods of time, for example using earth colors to evoke the Victorian era. The contrasts of a Greek façade, with multicolored architraves and balconies of turquoise and red, may seem like a riotous explosion, but in fact to use these hot colors in a composition can create a sense of harmony, serenity, and calm.

Color has an inherent ability to transform its surroundings. Our personal response to color lies deep within the psyche and defies explanation. Color can relate to personal experiences within us all.

An artist must search for a color that fits the sensation he or she experiences when viewing an object. It is not just a case of a green pitcher being the one shade of color, or even the one color. The eye is extremely sensitive, and capable of millions of decisions about color. Deciding on color is essentially selective observation and this power of color appreciation can be harnessed in the world of paint.

BELOW Nicholas Verrall, "Still Life with Enamel Pitchers" OIL. Subtle shifts in tone create a lively surface.

In the Dutch school, the use of similar tonal features was very deliberate. Artists would choose subjects of similar tones and color, for example a fish on a silver plate and a pewter mug with bread. Soft velvet light caressed the objects. All the tones run into each other to evoke a created landscape of related color.

Chiaroscuro is the dynamic use of light and shade. This method of elegant lighting, was used by Rembrandt (1606–1669), with objects, as if under a spotlight, looking almost solid. This strong contrast of lights and darks can bring to the still life a quality of melodrama, where highlighting is used to lead the viewer from one focal point to the next, and where

shadows cast in a certain way emphasize the shape of fruit or drapery, picking out surface texture.

Sfumato, from the Italian word meaning delicate shading, is the blurring of images for effect.

Leonardo da Vinci's (1452–1519) masterly use of paint, making soft transitions from light to dark, from shade to shade, creates this smoky, ambiguous effect. A softening of the edges of objects, and a

reduction of contrast as you travel further into the picture, can help create the illusion of depth and movement within the picture frame.

By treating still life as a learning experience, Matisse and Cézanne brought to the genre a combination of rhythmic brushstrokes and flattened perspective with decorative blocks of color to create a harmonious and balanced still life. The flat forms and bold color associated with these painters paved the way for the modern approach to paint.

Matisse's control of incredibly bright colors in his painting is due to an acute and sensitive knowledge of color relationships. His choice of palette, with madder, bright blues, and hot greens, is a prime example of how we may express ourselves through color.

ABOVE James McDonald, "Temptations 10/12" OIL. Dramatic use of contrast, light, and shade.

Blacks and whites

There are three whites commonly used in oil painting. Titanium white contains the dense pigment titanium dioxide, and it creates a good opaque base for mixing colors. It is fairly slow drying, and remains workable for a couple of days. Small amounts of titanium white will whiten any other color.

Zinc white, which has a slight blue tint to it, is more of a buttery texture and is the least opaque of the whites, with the slowest drying time. The transparent quality of zinc white makes it perfect for glazing paintings. It dries to a brittle, hard film.

Flake white, made of basic lead carbonate, is a very flexible paint to use. It is fast drying and suitable for underpainting.

Note that white does not appear on the watercolor palette. However, Chinese white, a form of zinc white, is often used for highlights and for adding body to color. With acrylic painting, titanium is again a good white to use. When using gouache, I prefer permanent white, which is an opaque, versatile liquid, capable of washes and solid highlights.

There are good blacks and grays available, but I personally do not use them, as I prefer to create my own by mixing other colors such as indigo and alizarin crimson. The depth of color that is created in this way can add an extra dimension to what might be a dull part of a painting.

COLOR

Uses of color

The overriding ability of color is to transform a picture into a painting, to excite a multitude of emotions, to inspire and invigorate. When color harmonies are achieved, the effects can be extraordinary.

Yellow is the color of spring; orange has reflections of fall. Limes or apples, with their acid greens, are excellent for vibrant contrasts with red. Look for the

**ABOVE Philip Sutton,
"Flowers from Pembrokeshire" OIL.
Decorative blocks of pure color to create
a balanced composition.**

greens and shapes of foliage that can enhance color composition. A bright color appears stronger when placed next to a neutral color such as a gray. Use color for mood: blue to denote sadness or despair, yellows for celebration. Many artists have been known for their obsession with color, notably

Van Gogh, who spent a whole summer in search of a specific yellow, or Picasso with his emotive "Blue Period."

Setting off forceful colors against each other, like the use of yellow and blue that Van Gogh favored, shows the power of color at its best. The intensity of the contrast may be tempered by the surface texture of the paint. Short, sharp, isolated brushstrokes of complementary color can optically built up with planes of color, giving objects a rugged, hefty form. The use of strong line competing with flat perspective can bring defined form to a composition.

Warm and cool colors

The color wheel (see below), and the separation of colors from warm to cool, is a useful tool in learning to understand the value of color. The warm colors, namely the yellows, reds, and oranges, are balanced by the cool range of greens, blues, and violets. You can use the color wheel to help create balance and harmony in placing colors. Try out a color combination that is two or three colors apart on the wheel.

ABOVE Philip Sutton, "Saskia's Flowers" OIL. The use of yellow and blue brought to full effect.

mix in the eye of the viewer to suggest a pure color; the strength of the combined color will be much more intense than if it had been mixed. This almost pointillist technique can be used to liven up small areas of the composition or to create dynamic contrasts over the whole surface. Henri Matisse said: "When you find three color tones near to each other ... let's say green, a violet, and a turquoise, their conjunction calls to mind a different color, and that is what we might call *the* color."

Color, pattern, and texture are important elements in any painting. Paint can be applied in clear, precise brushstrokes and

BELOW A color wheel showing that paint pigments may not correspond exactly to theoretical colors.

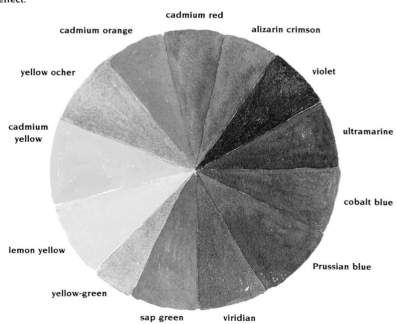

cadmium red
cadmium orange
alizarin crimson
yellow ocher
violet
cadmium yellow
ultramarine
cobalt blue
lemon yellow
Prussian blue
yellow-green
sap green
viridian

Complementary colors

To put the complementary colors of red and green against each other creates a contrast of the highest degree in color terms. These are the main complementary color contrasts, opposites on the color wheel: red–green; yellow–violet; orange–blue. When placed side by side in the painting, complementary colors fight for

ABOVE Philip Sutton,
"Calm was the Day" OIL.
The complementary colors of red and green bring the painting to life.

attention, creating a direct optical response and giving the painting a unique sense of vigor and energy.

Tiny amounts of a complementary color can transform a painting. You can control the

vibrancy of the area by adding more or less complementary color. A small amount of contrast can be appealing to the eye, but it can be uncomfortable if there is too much, with everything competing for attention. Using a contrast of colors that are not opposites on the color wheel gives more subtle nuances, while the dynamism of opposition is still present.

ABOVE Peter Graham,
"Theatrical Fruits" OIL.
Interplay of complementary colors
is an important compositional
element.

LEFT Sandy Murphy,
"Still Life Table" ACRYLIC.
Still life full of texture, pattern,
and color.

6

TECHNIQUES

iscovering the unique properties of different mediums is an exciting part of creating art. Form is simplified as soon as the brush touches the canvas, conveying subtle shifts in light and creating reflections and texture. The economical application of paint, of which Manet was master, can lead to extraordinarily fluent painting. Drawing and painting, using whatever medium, is about short cuts of visual imagery that persuade the viewer to see more than is actually there.

OILS

There are various ways to approach an oil painting. The paint can be heavily diluted or applied in thin coats to the canvas, or put on "alla prima," working wet-on-wet with vigorous, lively brushstrokes. Another approach is the building up of layers of wet on dry paint. Impasto and palette knife painting creates thick, jewel-like textures, while subdued tonal painting can project magnificent worlds beyond the canvas surface. You may find that a combination of different techniques leads you to the effect you are after.

Oil paint takes time to dry and this gives the artist the freedom to move the paint around the canvas. Scrape it off and wash carefully with turps—the paint is generally amenable to persuasion (unlike acrylic paint, which, once dried, will not budge!).

The oil painter's studio

Ideally the artist's studio should be an area that is separate from the rest of the house. Back bedrooms,

ABOVE Peter Graham, "Flight of Fancy Flowers"
Still life in oils.

BELOW Nicholas Verrall,
"Le Petit Dejeuner" OIL.
Beautiful use of light creates this
still life table.

sheds, or garages are usually the places you end up in! As long as you can keep the space dry, and warm in winter, and there is a good source of light, then you need look no further. I always work with the window open, to keep the air flowing and to reduce the fumes that oil paint produces.

A good easel is the main piece of furniture that you need. A radial

ABOVE Peter Graham, **"Harlequin Table Still Life"** OIL. **The still life table.**

studio easel is recommended. It can be tilted back and forth to suit the angle you wish to work at. A plain chest is invaluable, where papers, canvasses, drapes, and tools can all be accommodated.

You will need a sturdy small table to use for your still life setups, and a large table for all the equipment, palette, paints, brushes, and media.

Lightweight portable easels are useful for small work, but are not suitable for vigorous handling of paint. For convenience, I use a compact portable easel if I am outside in the garden or greenhouse.

Methods

The responsiveness of oil paint means that no two painters use the medium the same way. I will describe here some methods that you may want to try.

Using the *fat over lean* principle means adding more linseed to the turps/linseed mixture as you progress with the painting. Start with a mixture of mostly turps. This will dry quickly. Add more linseed for the subsequent layers so that they dry more slowly. This makes sure that earlier layers of paint do not dry after subsequent layers, which would cause cracking of the paint surface. A standard way to approach the technique is to make up fresh mixtures each day of linseed oil and English Distilled Turpentine, adding extra droplets of linseed oil each time. Keep a note of the number of droplets added.

Working *alla prima*, wet paint on wet, was the approach adopted by the French Impressionists in order to capture the essence of the moment. Often an *alla prima* painting is completed in one session, although you can work into the painting afterwards, tightening up color and shape or developing textures. The technique instills movement and vigor, employing energetic brushwork with strong strokes of broken color. When working with sunlight or shadow, *alla prima* painting is a good approach. Speed and accuracy of mark is necessary, and to develop these skills is a matter of practice. Don't be discouraged with poor results at first, because it takes a fair amount of development to begin to feel that you are getting somewhere.

The technique of glazing produces some of the most amazing effects possible with oil paint. It requires patience and planning ahead. Used extensively by the Renaissance painters, glazing is basically applying paint in thin transparent skins of color, to create a luminous and rich veneer. It can subtly change colors and tones without any distinct brushwork or use of strong color.

ABOVE James McDonald, "Two weeks Last Summer" OIL. A rich veneer created with glazes.

ABOVE Arthur Easton, "Still Life with Stone Jar, Pan, and Cloth" OIL. Arthur Easton uses the fat over lean method of applying the paint.

A personal approach

There are certain colors I have an affinity with, like shades of blue and green. I am inspired by the intoxicating colors of the Greek islands, the azure blue of the Mediterranean. I tend to choose subjects that reflect my own preference at the time (see page 82).

I lightly outline my still life composition on the canvas, using a mixture of titanium white and

ABOVE Peter Graham,
"Still Life with Teapot" OIL.
Alla prima painting capturing the moment.

lemon yellow hue. I may suggest the colors of objects with very diluted paint (see page 83). I block in general areas of background and rough shapes of the objects, using a large flat or filbert bristle brush and lots of diluted color, and wiping any drips with a cotton cloth

(page 82). As I build up color, shape, and shadow, I gradually add more linseed to my mixture of paint and turps, using the traditional method of "fat over lean." I apply the paint in a fluid manner, altering structure as I go along. In general I am not too worried about discipline of style, and I have often finished a painting with some roughly treated areas, which contrast with detailed patterns or objects.

BLACK VASE AND APPLES

Painting in oils

PETER GRAHAM

With a vibrant palette of colors, Peter Graham captures the pattern, color, and contrast of this still life arrangement.

PALETTE

Lemon yellow hue: Winsor lemon: cadmium yellow: aureolin: Naples yellow: terra rosa: raw umber: alizarin crimson: cadmium red: cadmium scarlet: permanent rose: cobalt violet: French ultramarine: indigo: cadmium green: Winsor green: Prussian green: titanium white.

1 A patterned drape with blues and browns frames a composition where delightfully intense colors and the natural shapes of fruit and flowers, with a reflective vase at their center, provide an exciting subject to paint.

2 Using a large, flat bristle brush (no. 12) and lots of turps, the general colors and shades are loosely blocked in. No great attention is paid to detail at this early stage in the painting.

3 More precise brushmarks are employed to create shapes within the flowers. Violet and terra rosa are used for the darker areas within the composition. Care is taken not to create too strong a contrast between objects at this point.

4 The full spectrum of color is now roughly painted, giving a good idea of how the composition is going to end up.

5 A cloth is used to wipe any unwanted paint off the canvas.

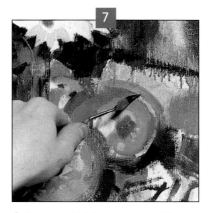

6 I start to tighten up composition and build up color with slightly thicker paint. Incidental shapes such as the pattern in the foreground are introduced.

7 A painting knife is used to scrape an outline around the apple, revealing the ground color while defining the round shape of the fruit.

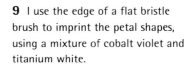

8 At this stage the fruit is suggested by color rather than by detail.

9 I use the edge of a flat bristle brush to imprint the petal shapes, using a mixture of cobalt violet and titanium white.

12 The negative shapes between the petals of the flowers are given a very dark color to produce a strong contrast. Indigo and Prussian green have been applied in these areas.

10 Here I use a fan brush to blend the dark tone and light tone together, creating a smooth transition and giving the fruit a three-dimensional feel.

11 The handle of a brush can be useful. Here it has been used to create a texture on the orange cloth, to emphasize and contrast with the polished surface of the apple.

13 The finished work is a highly colored composition, with natural tones, and shapes that combine detailed brushwork with looser, more fluid strokes.

ABOVE A palette knife is ideal for mixing color.

I avoid mixing the color on the painting itself. This should be done on a large palette and preferably with a painting knife (see left). Using a large palette gives you space to allow the various mixtures to remain in the palette for a period of time. This is helpful for color matching or for using more of the same color. Always mix more color than you need. You never know if it will come in handy at later stages in the painting.

When the majority of the painting is developed to the point where strong shape and form are evident, I work on the delicate color changes, for example where light reflects on fruit or a polished coffeepot. I incorporate detail using small flat brushes or sables.

If I am concerned with the buildup of paint or muddying of color on the canvas, I use the technique known as tonking (see Chapter 8) to remove excess paint. I may, from time to time, use a painting knife for sgraffito work (see Chapter 8), creating outline and scraped texture where I feel it can add to the overall balance of the composition.

ABOVE Peter Graham, "Art Deco Table" Still life in oils. Bold colors combined with careful attention to detail.

WATERCOLORS

The most traditional British medium is the watercolor. The delights of working with the delicate washes and freshness of color make watercolor still life one of the most relaxing and satisfying pursuits. Watercolor can reveal the fleeting nature of flowers and light with careful overlays of color, and is capable of creating remarkable depth and intensity. Rendering the bloom on a peach or the translucent skin on an apple, watercolor has an ethereal quality that transcends all.

Cézanne was able to capture reflected light with his fragmented brushwork and transparent glazes. He would often employ the actual surface of the paper as a tone in his painting. With a few carefully placed transparent washes of color and gestural brushmarks, he would leave the white of the paper largely untouched, thereby allowing the full expressiveness of his subject to shine through. He was one of the few painters in history who found, through watercolor, answers to problems of composition and expressiveness, form and outline.

ABOVE Ronald Jesty, "Red Mullets"
WATERCOLOR. **A fresh approach creating
dramatic shapes with subtle washes.**

The incredible versatility of this
transparent medium is one of the
reasons why it is so attractive to
the artist. Painting in watercolor
requires discipline and patience.
In order to understand the
properties of different colors, it is
worth doing a series of washes with
each color to find out how they
handle. Some colors, Prussian blue
for instance, are very potent, and a

tiny amount of paint goes a long
way. Overlaying one transparent
wash on to the next yields quite
subtle results and can give
tremendous depth to a painting.

The quality of the paper is crucial
when painting in watercolor,
because the white of the paper
often becomes the white of the
painting. The tooth of a paper can
be used by the painter to turn a
series of strokes into descriptive
textured surfaces; for example by
dragging a brush full of color over a
rough paper to describe the surface
of an orange or lemon, so that the
paint can pick out and exaggerate
the surface of the paper.

Methods
Watercolor is applied from light to
dark. Adjusting to a paint that
essentially has no white requires
careful planning for composition. In
practice, the use of Chinese white
or gouache paint can achieve light
on dark, but the purists prefer to
leave the white paint out. When
working watercolor you can darken
areas but generally it is difficult to
lighten areas. If you are used to
working with oil or gouache,
changing to watercolor takes some
getting used to, but once you are
familiar with the transparent
properties of the medium it is an
enjoyable way of painting.

**ABOVE Shirley Trevena,
"Blue Fruit Bowl" WATERCOLOR.
The white of the paper brought to full
effect in the final painting.**

Wash techniques, using the wonderful array of mops and brushes available, make this medium one of the most entertaining. The spontaneous effect and the random nature of wet paint can lead to happy accidents that bring a painting to life.

Watercolor washes reveal and conceal; they can bind the painting elements together. A natural sponge can create excellent effects. Dabbing the sponge on wet washes can lift areas of color successfully. The sponge can also be used to apply paint for scumbling.

what kind of effects you achieve. With watercolor, lighter tones are obtained by thinning the colors with water, and when working wet-on-wet the bleeding of one color leads to unique gradations of tones and hues.

The classic technique of working wet-on-dry produces the extraordinary results of inner light that watercolor is associated with. It can involve building up a series of layers, allowing each to dry in turn, leading to a highly polished finish.

The beauty of white paper is its ability to shine through layers of watercolor paint. Be careful not to overwork the painting, as this sensitive medium can become dull and lifeless through overpainting.

Watercolor inks are also worth experimenting with. They can achieve a brilliantly colored image. They are used similarly to watercolor, except that they need to be heavily diluted with water, because they are highly concentrated. The use of pencil over the dried ink can be very effective in pulling forms together.

ABOVE Oliver Soskice, "Still Life with Pears" Delicate use of broken color.

Wax or masking fluid can be employed to preserve the white of the paper. First, you paint the wax or fluid over the areas of the paper that you want to stay clear. When washes are laid over wax, the resulting motley texture can be very appealing. The difference between wax and masking fluid is that the wax is not removed from the paper, while masking fluid rubs off with the finger when it is safe to reveal the white paper underneath!

Working wet-on-wet allows watercolor to be used to its full unique effect. The term means using wet paint on a wet paper, or wet paint added to wet paint. This way of working is unpredictable, but its random nature holds excitement for the painter. The only way to learn how colors react with this method is to try out different papers and levels of wetness to see

ABOVE Shirley Trevena, "Hot Daffodils"
Intensity of color can be achieved with
watercolor.

STILL LIFE TABLE

Watercolor with gold

JENNY WHEATLEY

This still life in watercolors and gold by Jenny Wheatley shows how washes and detail can combine to produce that distinctive luminous quality unique to this medium.

ABOVE Jenny's palette and brushes.

PALETTE

Schmincke Watercolors: Naples yellow: permanent yellow light: Indian yellow: yellow ocher: vermilion: English red light: permanent red deep: brilliant purple: carmine: cerulean blue: cobalt blue: permanent violet: brilliant blue: ultramarine blue: ultramarine violet: opaque green light: May green: green lake deep: brilliant turquoise: gold metallic powder.

1 This ornate arrangement presents wonderful possibilities for exploring color and contour.

2 The paper is stretched, then the composition is carefully drawn, using pencil line and no shading.

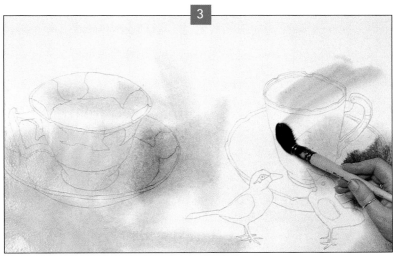

3 Using a wet-on-wet technique and working on a dampened surface, a no. 7 Raphael squirrel mop is used to load on color with large, generous brushstrokes. All the time, the artist is referring to the objects for tone and color that relate to the composition.

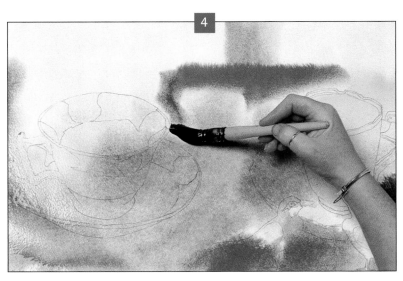

4 This creates a multicolored background, which gradually soaks into the paper and merges one color into the next. The artist works quickly in order to allow this to happen.

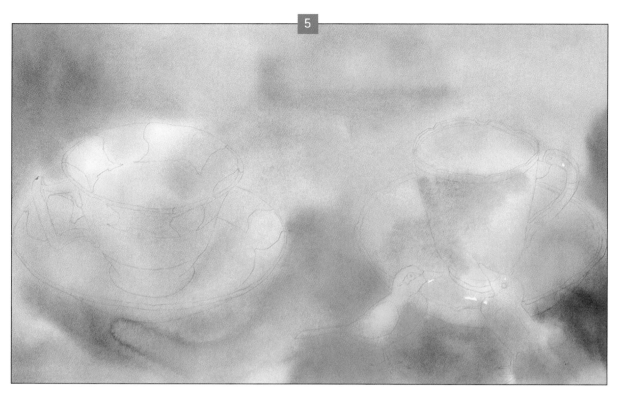

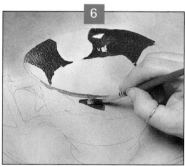

5 Now that the background is complete, it is left to dry. Note that areas left white, or with just a hint of yellow, are where the highlights of the painting will eventually fall.

6 The detail is now added, using a no. 6 round sable. Ultramarine blue and violet are used to build up the pattern on the cup.

7 Painting one object nearly to a finish allows the artist to gauge the effect of the luminous quality of the underlying washes.

9 The buildup of pattern unifies the composition.

10 The pattern on the cloth is balanced by the intricately detailed cups.

11 As a final touch, gold metallic powder is dabbed on with a soft cloth to enhance areas of the painting.

8 Darker washes are applied, allowing some of the under color to show through. The random nature of watercolor is brought to full

advantage here, especially where the yellows washes sit beautifully, giving the ornamental bird a brilliant glow.

12 Gold is used to pick out the highlights on the edge of the saucer.

13 The finished painting demonstrates how watercolor can produce wonderful effects of reflected light, combined with exquisite pattern and detail.

GOUACHE

Gouache, or designer's gouache, holds the properties of watercolor coupled with an opaque capability. This medium is able to produce flat areas of pure color as well as gradation of tone, and is excellent for both the beginner and the experienced painter.

A good approach when using gouache is to start a still life using washes to block in the composition. Synthetic flats and bristle brushes can be excellent at this early stage. As the work develops, employ the more opaque qualities of the paint.

Protecting areas of light color are just as important as with watercolor, except that you can paint over and alter your marks. This ability to cover up layers of paint can be very helpful for the beginner searching for a satisfactory composition.

With a little PVA glue in your mix of water, you can achieve superb glazes. Gum Arabic, applied at the latter stages, can add a gloss to the paint and give the colors more vibrancy. Bristle brushes and sables are suitable for applying the paint, but sponges and a toothbrush are useful tools to create that extra dimension in textured marks.

The use of gouache on tinted paper can have startling effects, mainly due to the opacity of the paint, and when coupled with watercolor, this can produce wonderfully expressive results.

ACRYLIC

Acrylic paints are an exciting alternative to paint with. Acrylic is a compatible medium. It can be applied to most absorbent surfaces, including canvas, paper, and board.

TOP Jenny Wheatley, "Tropical Garden" Watercolor, pastel, dye PVA glue, and gouache are all used here.

LEFT Sandy Murphy, "The Blue Mirror" Vigorous brushed textures and patterns using acrylics.

ABOVE James McDonald, "Janets Jar"
Control that can be achieved with acrylic paint.

As it is a water-soluble paint, paper should be stretched or sealed before acrylic is applied. There are excellent acrylic canvas boards and painting pads available.

It is important to familiarize yourself with the various mediums and their effects. Most of these create superb variations for glazes, impasto technique or washes, and this flexibility can lift your spirits.

With its fast-drying properties, acrylic lends itself to glazes, since these involve building up the surface with several layers. Unlike with watercolor, this process can reveal results very quickly. Some artists use a hair dryer to speed up the drying process.

EGG TEMPERA

The traditional technique of egg tempera was used until the end of the 15th century, and it is experiencing a revival today. This water-based medium uses the binding properties of egg yolk to complete the mixture of pigment.

The traditional ground to work on is wooden board, primed with several coats of gesso. The white of the gesso shines through the tempera to enhance the reflected light.

Egg tempera has the ability to produce luminous, transparent glazes, and due to its fast-drying properties, it allows tones and shades to be built up very subtly. With its sticky and fast-drying nature, tempera has to be applied using short brushstrokes, and it resists blending.

PASTEL

Working with pastel can be a tremendous way into the world of art, because you can achieve brilliance of color combined with excellent drawing capabilities. Pastel has the ability to create areas of pure color or texture and crosshatching, as well as producing subtle blending of tone.

Some artists refer to pastel work as "painting," due to the layering effect that can be built up and the deep, rich textures that can be developed. It can be difficult to distinguish such a work from a painting when pastels are used to full effect.

When building up a pastel still life, lightly sketch in the lights and darks, then, as you gradually establish the composition, become firmer with your mark. Pastel works well over a watercolor wash or on tinted papers. Think about using tinted paper that is sympathetic to the color of your composition: for example, a warm brown tint may enhance a still life containing terracotta pots.

Try not to use up the "tooth" of the paper too early, for this causes clogging, preventing the paper from

BELOW David Napp,
"Flower Still Life with Peaches" PASTEL.
Bold use of pastel.

accepting any more pastel. Some artists work on sandpaper, which allows one to add layer after layer without filling up the tooth of the paper.

A hint to stop pastels rolling off your work surface is to tape a piece of corrugated cardboard onto your table and lay the pastel sticks on it. This keeps them from disappearing over the edge and breaking on the floor! It is worth while keeping all the little bits of pastel that you end up with, as they can come in handy for highlights and small marks that you might want to make. Pastel sticks can be cleaned by agitating in a bowl of dry rice!

ABOVE David Napp, "Moroccan Still Life" PASTEL.
Dynamic perspective with strong pattern.

TOP Derek Daniells,
"Garden Flowers" PASTEL.
A corner of the garden holds
great inspiration.

LEFT David Napp,
"Clarice Cliff Pots and
Thai Silks" PASTEL.
The impact of the intense
color.

ABOVE David Napp, "Provencal Provisions" PASTEL.
A strong drawing element and use of perspective.

7

GOOD WORKING PRACTICES

O ne of the biggest problems an artist faces is to keep working and practicing. Find out what time of day or night suits your mood, and give yourself a routine to follow. Set aside specific hours for your painting at the studio. Set yourself achievable goals.

DISCIPLINE OF WORKING

Part of the discipline in the studio must be the ongoing process of keeping all the equipment immaculately clean. Keep a good supply of clean cotton rags for cleaning brushes, as well as for catching a drip or removing unwanted paint.

It is a good idea to paint the studio once a year as this forces you to clean out all those corners that collect assortments of bottles, boards, and old paint cans. A thorough coat of white paint livens up a dull wall and also gets rid of all those paint splatters that have accumulated from a year's worth of painting.

BELOW Peter Graham, **"Magical Apples Still Life"** OIL. **The interplay of color and pattern create an exciting composition.**

TOP Peter Graham,
"Still Life with Tulips" OIL.
Capturing the delicate fleeting
nature of flowers.

LEFT Shirley Trevena,
"Still Life with Fruit and Vegetables"
An evocative kitchen scene
in watercolor.

CHANGING LIGHT

When working with natural light, the problem of changing contrast is ongoing. Try to set up the still life at the point in your studio where there is the most diffuse light. Find the spot where the least amount of direct light falls. As the seasons unfold, the area in the studio with the least direct light will change. Think about taking advantage of this by moving your working positions throughout the year.

PRIMING AND SIZING

Acrylic gesso is a suitable ground to paint on when working with oil and acrylic. The acrylic gesso primer can be applied in two or three coats. Alternatively, you can use the traditional method of sizing with rabbit-skin glue. Size seals the surface pores, making the support less absorbent. This stops the oil in the paint layers from seeping into the canvas, leaving the paint surface to crack and flake. Glue size is made by mixing water with the dry granules of glue and heating very gently.

When applying size or primer, always use a top quality interior decorator's brush; low-quality one may shed bristles onto the painting. For most purposes, a 2-inch bristle brush will be suitable. To create a surface texture, apply the primer, and then carefully press a piece of textured cloth such as a heavy-duty canvas into the wet paint and peel off slowly. The texture will then be imprinted.

ABOVE Sandy Murphy, "Rose Table" MIXED MEDIA.
Lighting is integral to the composition.

THE PALETTE

It is best to set out your paints in groups of colors: for example, a blue group of French ultramarine, cobalt blue, indigo, and cerulean blue. Next to them you can place the purples or greens. Sticking to the order of the color wheel is a good rule to follow.

Adding new paint in the same place on the palette has many advantages, most importantly, being able to find a color instantly; you will know where each color lies (see below).

With oils, it is generally not necessary to clean the main palette as you go along, provided that you leave enough room around each of your colors for mixing. The mixtures can help with color balancing as you advance through the painting. If they are cleaned immediately, you lose this reference, and you may find it difficult to mix the same color again.

TOP Peter Graham,
"The Magical Table"
Color balance throughout the composition
is very important.

LEFT "The Oil Painter's Palette."
Where the arrangement of colors
is permanent.

CARE OF BRUSHES

It is crucially important to take care of your brushes. They can be the most expensive part of the artist's equipment, and the most sensitive to adverse conditions. With watercolor and gouache, always rinse brushes with cold water under the faucet when possible, to ensure the pigment is completely removed. If a brush contains some dried pigment, agitate it in a jar of warm water with a little Ivory liquid.

An important thing to remember when using acrylics is never to let the paint dry on the brush. If this happens the brush will be ruined. When painting, have a container of water to rest brushes in until they are needed again, and clean brushes with warm soapy water.

Clean oil brushes meticulously, but gently, with white spirit and a soft cotton rag, the softer the better. Have a small pot of artist's white spirit by the easel to immerse the brush in. Change your cleaning mixture as soon as it turns into a muddy gray. Try not to leave a brush sitting headfirst in the pot. When finished for the day, always wash brushes with soap and water to prolong their life.

After cleaning sable brushes, take care to reshape the tip. This can be done with your fingers and a little saliva. A suitable method to store all brushes, with their bristles up, is in a pitcher or old coffeepot.

Much of the wear in a brush occurs during the mixing process. A brush can easily get ruined if the mixing of color is not done methodically and carefully. For this very reason, some oil painters use a palette knife for mixing. If you prefer to mix paint with a brush, use an old one, and save the good brushes for the real job of applying

ABOVE Arthur Easton, "Onions, Enamelled Jug and Withered Roses" OIL. A still life with center piece of dried flowers.

the paint! The outer hairs on a bristle brush gradually get shorter and shorter, and the brush takes on a more pointed shape. The sable brush should never be used to mix oil or acrylic color. The hairs on the sable can become splayed and fall out. Note that when working with sable brushes, great care should be taken not to allow a buildup of paint at the heel of the brush. The paint must be cleaned from the brush so as not to sully the next

color. Ongoing careful cleaning of all brushes cannot be stressed enough.

Synthetic brushes must be treated with care too. They will lose their shape if they are manipulated in awkward directions. Try not to overload any brush, as this will alter its shape and it will not perform properly.

CARE OF FLOWERS AND FRUIT

Working with cut flowers can wreck your plans. Wilting and withering flowers are a headache for the artist! Speed and immediate perception of color, combined with coordination of hand and eye, are needed. Accurate detail is not as important for the painter as it is for the botanist. The artist can succeed in giving an impression of a hundred petals with just a few deft brushstrokes. Remember that painting a picture slowly or quickly has nothing whatsoever to do with whether it is a good or a bad painting. If you are attempting to paint delicate flowers, concentrate on the shape and texture of them at the earliest possible moment in your painting.

If flower stems were not put in water as soon as they were cut, they must be re-cut, or they will dry out and will not take up water readily. Cut the stems at an angle. This gives the flower a larger area in

which to take up water. Remove any leaves that will be below water level in the vase. Don't arrange the still life in a breezy area.

If possible, stand flowers overnight in a pail of water before arranging them. Changing the water in the vase every two days will prolong the life of the flowers. With roses, cut the stem at an angle and split the stem, and remove thorns below the water level.

It helps to balance a composition if you work with threes or fives with flowers and fruit, and the more random the arrangement, the more interesting to the eye. As a general rule, the height of your flower arrangement should be

around one-and-a-half times the size of the vase or container.

When you are painting food and flowers, especially in the summer, you need to work fast. Keep the area around the still life table clean, and spray with insect repellent. When buying fruit try under-ripe, hard fruit, which will have a longer life. Hard fruits such as apples, lemons or oranges will last, but peaches or other soft fruits can cause problems.

**BELOW Philip Sutton,
"Flowers for Claude Sutton"
Still life with fruit and flowers in oils.**

8

EXPANDING YOUR SKILLS

Whatever medium you choose, there are always ways of developing and furthering your skills. Whether you take from a past tradition or adopt some of the more recent techniques, testing yourself is really essential for the newcomer as well as the serious artist. Learning more about the processes involved in painting, and understanding more about what you can and can't do with paint, will enhance your enjoyment of still life.

Keeping an experimental element to your work is a good approach to adopt, although it has its drawbacks. You may leave a lot of paintings by the wayside. In the long term, though, this is better than to paint with a safe formula within set parameters, which can often lead to stiff, lifeless work.

SGRAFFITO AND SCRAPING BACK

Sgraffito, to scrape away paint, was a technique employed extensively by Rembrandt. It is particularly useful for drawing into oil paint to suggest shape and form (see left). Using a palette knife or painting knife, one can create interesting textures and outlines. This is an excellent method of defining objects, and it brings in an element of drawing to a composition. The technique involves drawing through a wet layer of paint to reveal another layer underneath, or to take the surface back to the ground color. The side of the palette knife can be used for scraping back and removing large sections of paint, leaving a textured finish below. A common technique employed to strengthen form is to use the end of the brush to score into an impasto paint. Combs, forks, or any rigid instrument can be used to scratch into the paint to create texture. It is, however, best to avoid scratching into dry paint, for this may damage the canvas.

LEFT "Anemones" OIL, **detail by Peter Graham. A painting knife has been used to create the texture on the orange drape and pick out the edge of the jug.**

TONKING

This technique can be very useful for oil painters. When an area becomes overloaded with paint, this is the best way of reducing the amount of paint without disturbing the underlying structure of what has been laid down. To clear an excess of wet paint, place a sheet of newsprint over the overloaded area and rub gently until the paint has absorbed into the paper. Slowly peel off the paper (see below). This will have absorbed the oil in the paint, to reveal the area as a thinned-down version of the original thick painted surface. This allows you to continue working without muddying the colors.

BELOW Tonking. Excess paint being lifted off the canvas by absorbing on to newspaper.

GLAZES

Glazing is a method of laying one thin wash of color over another so that each layer modifies the one below. Glazes are very thin, so that light can travel through and be reflected back. This gives them their luminous quality.

A transparent layer of color laid over another (see page 113) can bring wonderful glowing areas of inner light to your work. It is best to mix on a white surface, such as a sheet of glass placed over white paper. You may also find that application with a soft brush, as opposed to a hog bristle brush, is much more suitable. The color underneath will shine through, reflecting the light through the transparent layer.

It is well worth doing some glazing experiments with colors. To increase the intensity of a red, for example, lay a strong yellow ground, and build up glazes of red. The resulting color will be brighter and more luminous than if the red paint had been applied on its own. Glazing can also be useful for dulling down areas of a painting that jump out at you. A thin glaze of a neutral color can reduce the intensity of a strong color underneath.

Glazes are achievable with water-based paints as well as with oil, and there are various glazing mediums available to help the transparency and flow of paint. With pastel you can create a glazing effect by applying thin lines of a second color like a veil over the ground color. The colors then mix optically. The technique allows the artist to subtly change tone without disturbing the overall composition and form of the work.

ACRYLIC GLAZE

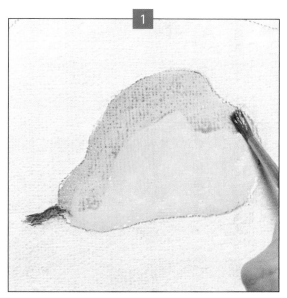

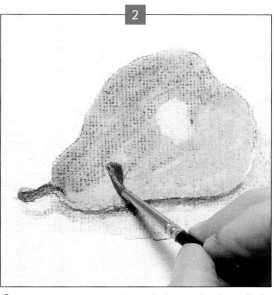

1 The ground color of Azo yellow light is painted and left to dry. Then an initial thin coat of French ultramarine is applied.

2 Another transparent glaze of ultramarine is applied. After each stage, the work is left to dry. You can see the original layers reflecting through.

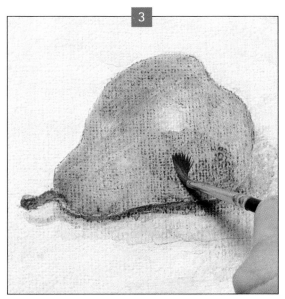

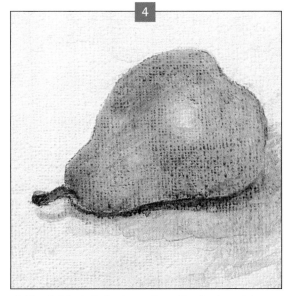

3 Areas of shadow are given a glaze using naphthol crimson, enhancing the three-dimensional aspect of the fruit.

4 The finished study shows the veils of color, giving depth and gloss to the surface of the fruit.

SPLATTERING

To capture the energy of paint and brushwork, a splattering of paint can be very effective (see below). In the early stages of an oil or watercolor painting, using a large bright or flat hog bristle and a thinned mixture of paint, I energetically imprint the bristles on the support, sending droplets of paint cascading over the painting. I find this is an excellent way to bring movement into the underpainting. There are various other ways of achieving a splattering effect, including using an old toothbrush as well as drawing a thumb across the bristles, thus creating superb localized fine spots, randomly dispersed; or tapping one brush loaded with paint over another.

BELOW Splattering thinned paint for effect.

SCUMBLING

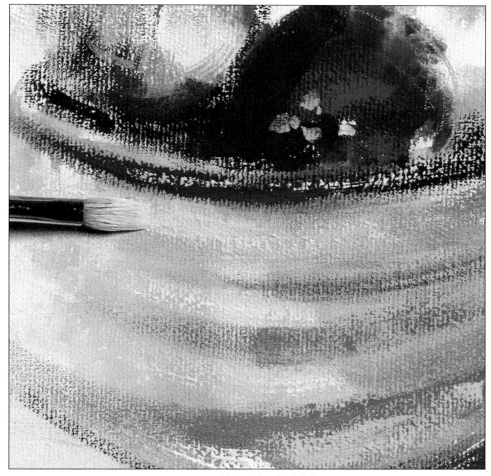

ABOVE Scumbling with a flat bristle brush to create texture.

The dry-brush technique known as scumbling (see above) can achieve both depth and texture to the painting at the same time. This involves working over a dry color with a dry brush and just a little color, allowing the base color to show through in parts. It is advisable to use a durable brush like a hog bristle to scrub one color on top of another. Scumbling techniques help produce rich textures and luminous colors and tones to the painting.

REFLECTED LIGHT

Using the white of the canvas can give painting a luminous quality. Light can reflect back through layers of paint. A superb method of "drawing" objects can be simply to leave some of the white primed canvas showing through at the right places. When working against sunlight this can be particularly effective, allowing the white canvas to shine through and enhance all the contrasts.

Some artists prefer to coat the whole canvas with a tone, such as an ocher or sienna color, and allow this color to permeate and reflect back through their painting. Using a colored ground to reflect light can have a strong unifying effect on the whole composition.

ABOVE Petula Stone, "Strawberries"
A luminous quality achieved with watercolor glazes.

TOP Shirley Trevena,
"Red Pears"
The white of the paper
helps create the composition.

LEFT Philip Sutton,
"Apple Blossom"
The canvas ground shines
through the paint bringing
a sense of inner light.

LEFT Blending color with fingers can achieve good results.

BELOW The yellow plate and lemons contrast with the shadow area of violet.

FINGER PAINTING

Although this may appear clumsy, there are times when fingers (see above) do the best job. The fingers are sensitive "tools," and many of the great masters used their fingers to manipulate the surface of their paintings, among them Leonardo da Vinci and Goya. Fingers can soften line and smooth the change of tone, and can rub paint into the grain of the canvas. To achieve a similar sensitivity while keeping the paint off the fingers, wrap a piece of cotton rag tightly around the finger and then treat the surface of the painting as if you were polishing silver.

LIVENING UP SHADOWS

Building up color in shadow helps bring to life dull areas of a painting. Complementary colors, those at the opposite sides of the wheel (red–green, blue–orange, yellow–violet), can be played off each other for effect. The juxtaposition of tiny amounts of these opposite colors can create vibrant contrasts that can transform a painting; for example yellow and violet could be the right contrast to lift an area (see right).

IMPASTO

Thickening oil paint by mixing with impasto mediums can produce very satisfying textures, and can add great weight to brushstrokes and energy to textures (see right). The buttery consistency of oil paint lends itself to this approach. The use of a fast-drying alkyd medium helps reduce the cracking tendency of thick paint. Thick mixtures of color tend to dull and muddy if you work them too long on the canvas, so keep the painting fresh and plan your marks if you possibly can.

A stout bristle brush such as a filbert can get the best response from a thickened paint. Palette and painting knives are suitable tools for mixing and applying paint and creating ridges and textures. Combs and even pieces of cardboard add to the variety of impasto textures that can be produced. Plaster or decorator's filler give a fine-grained consistency to undiluted oil paint. Adding sand will give a grainy texture. Experiment with adding sawdust for a texture of brown sugar, or wood chips for a flaky appearance.

TOP John Yardley, "White Roses + Pewter" Exquisite use of light.

BELOW Oil paint mixed with oleopasto allows the artist to develop impasto textures.

MIXED MEDIA

The term "mixed media" refers to all works that use more than one medium. Artists can combine ink, gouache, acrylic, and pastel, employing the best qualities of each medium. This method of working can be very expressive, getting around the limitations of one medium by exploiting the qualities of another! Mixed media gives the artist great freedom of expression and can produce tremendous results (see below).

Pastel with gouache or watercolor is a very compatible combination of mediums. Indian inks, oil pastels, pencil, charcoal, and conté are all worth considering in the discovery process to find the approach that suits you. Colored pencils, especially the water-soluble kind, can create textural contrasts with gouache. The use of soft pastel over flat, opaque areas of acrylic or gouache paint can be very effective. The surface of gouache is especially good for working on with pastel. The paint has a slightly rough texture when dry, which picks up the soft pastel beautifully. Oil pastel and even oil paint can be used on top of water-based mediums, but not the other way around, as the paint will often not settle.

The use of acrylic for underpainting is a technique employed by many oil painters, as this layer will dry rapidly and allow you to work up your picture in a short space of time. This is a useful approach when painting flowers or foods that don't last long.

BELOW "Red Onions" MIXED MEDIA, by Petula Stone. Here Petula has used a white oil pastel resist, then overlaid with watercolor ink washes. The onions are drawn using oil pastel, and then an overall surface texture was created, using white gouache and scumbling with a dry brush.

TOP Sandy Murphy, "White Tulips"
Acrylic and ink with oil pastel for highlights.

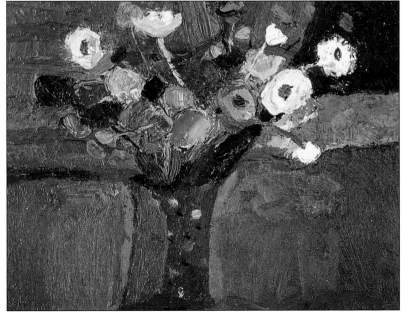

LEFT Sandy Murphy, "The Blue Vase"
Impasto technique of applying the paint.

9

PRESENTATION AND CARE OF WORKS

A rt should revive the spirit and instill emotions. It should invigorate and entertain. Still life can speak quietly but say great things. Presentation and framing play an important part in creating and enhancing the impact of a work of art.

Many artists feel that once the painting is complete, the frame is an afterthought. You must forget this myth, especially if you are thinking of entering work for an art contest or exhibition. A well-made and well-designed frame can enhance and exemplify your work to a degree that would surprise even the most imaginative person. The type of mount and molding should be in empathy with the painting itself. It should complement without calling attention to itself.

FRAMING

When selecting moldings or mounts, the expertise of your framer comes into play. Of course, it is possible to make your own frames and put effort into staining and coloring them, but finding a sympathetic framer will benefit you greatly. When you are working with paint or pastel, time spent at the easel is the best way to use your energies, and to take on the job of frame maker as well as painter will give you an uphill struggle.

When mounting work, I prefer to use a mount that is at least three inches wide. I tend to use off-white shades of mounting board. Mounts and/or washes over different colored mounting boards can pull out certain colors within your composition.

The fascinating techniques involved in preparing frames, each style a craft in itself, take time to master. A good frame maker is like gold dust, so it is worth looking at a number of framers to find one whose work you like. Keep your eyes open for framers who produce exclusive designs and decoration.

The choice of decorated moldings is vast: period frames, such as Italian moldings, richly

ABOVE Peter Graham, "Deco Fruits" OIL. 20 x 16 inches A "whistler" frame with gold tipped edges.

decorated with engraving and sgraffito effects, swept moldings, flat moldings, or reverse moldings. Frames that are hand colored are more expensive, but the results can be worth it.

The delicate nature of watercolor demands a refined and sympathetic style of mount and frame. A traditional method of presenting watercolor paintings is to have a wide mount incorporating line and wash decoration. Double-thickness mounts are also excellent for giving

more depth to the painting itself. The advantage of double mounts is that the window effect of the mount is strengthened, allowing more depth to be created under the glass. Remember to always use acid-free papers and boards.

Gilt frames are very expensive, but the use of gold and silver leaf in frame making can achieve tremendous results. There are cheaper alternatives, such as metal leaf in silver and gold, which give a similar glint to a frame. Remember that the picture frame has to fit it with the environment in which the painting will eventually hang, so think about the style carefully. Paintings are often reframed by a new owner.

ABOVE Jeremy Galton, "Lilies in a Blue Vase" OIL. 20 x 15½ inches
Framed using a mount with line washes, glass and a distressed gold frame.

When framing oil paintings, the use of a small wooden or canvas slip is popular. This has a similar effect to that of a mount. It separates the canvas from the frame, and gives a sense of depth to the whole framed work.

The glass used for framing is normally ⅛ inch thick. Some artists prefer to glaze oil paintings. This physically protects the surface from any damage and the effects of the environment, but oils do not really need glass to look their best.

PRESENTATION

When putting works on a wall, think about arranging in groups and integrating them with their surroundings. Pick out styles of frame that reflect architectural features, and use the edges of a piece of furniture to guide you in selecting appropriate widths for a painting that could be hung above: for example, match up the sides of a sideboard with a painting. It is a good approach to hang work with the center of the picture at eye level.

There are basically two ways of hanging paintings, an ordered symmetrical fashion or an informal fashion. Geometrical ordered arrangements could mean a series of pictures all lined up level at the tops, with a standard gap between each, or hung in a square format with all outside edges in line. This system of hanging works best when the pictures are all the same size. A column of pictures will accentuate the height of a room, and a horizontal run of pictures will give a room more width.

When deciding how to hang an unusually shaped canvas or when filling narrow walls, an informal approach is useful. Experiment to find the most appealing arrangement. Large pictures need room to breathe, while smaller works hang well in clusters.

Avoid hanging work above a central heating radiator. Rising heat can dry out and warp a frame or damage a painting. In general, paintings should not be hung in direct sunlight.

BELOW Peter Graham, "Guernsey Roses" OIL. 26 x 32 inches A heavy scoop frame hand finished with gold highlights.

CARE OF YOUR WORK

Framed paintings, when not on display, take up a remarkable amount of space, and are easily damaged if they are not well protected. It is a good idea to cover them with bubble wrap if you are planning to store work for a while, as this both protects and insulates the work. Store paintings in a dry part of the house, which has a fairly constant temperature and not much traffic! This prevents the warping of stretchers and frames, the development of mold, and accidental damage. A garage is not a suitable spot, especially in the winter.

You can always tell an artist's house because they hang their own paintings everywhere. They take up only wall space, and there is the added advantage that the greater public gets to look at them!

BELOW Nicholas Verrall, "The Library" OIL ON BOARD. **A beautifully painted still life interior.**

INDEX